GHOSTS WALK!

Autobiography of a Medium and Spiritual Teacher

Gladys Franklin

Soul Lore

Feed thou my lambs

JOHN 21:15

CONTENTS

FOREWORD

Gladys Franklin was born in 1909, before the First World War. From an early age she saw and heard spirit visitors objectively, which is to say with her eyes open. She later became well known as a medium and a healer, only to find that her ardent desire to know the full truth of life went unsatisfied. Her subsequent journey towards understanding and experiencing a greater awareness of the inner self and the soul, teaching others to do the same, is what you will read about in this book.

I was first introduced to Gladys in the autumn of 1970, when my father and I enrolled in her classes for spiritual enlightenment. My original impression was that of a very knowledgeable, inspirational person, whose overriding aura of sincerity and friendliness embraced everyone she met. Over the next thirty years she was to become my teacher, mentor, friend, and in many respects like a second mum. Even after three decades, including quite a number of years living in the same household, my original impression never changed, for she was always the example of what she taught.

Throughout her life Gladys was a prolific writer. She wrote about her frequent out-of-body and sleepstate experiences, and how by virtue of them she gained a deep insight into the whys and wherefores of life and death.

At three distinct points in her life Gladys wrote what might be loosely termed an autobiography. In my role as editor I have merged what were three separate texts into this single volume. Over the time span during which these autobiographies were written Gladys adopted a writing style that altered with her ever-increasing knowledge and understanding, but I have made no attempt to 'update' any of her wording or terminology, or to otherwise change the style associated with any particular phase of her teaching.

Before going any further, I would like to pass on the advice that Gladys gave about reading, and that is not to skim or to rush through the words like reading a newspaper. Savour the words; allow them to register with your consciousness. Not only is this an account of Gladys' life, it also embodies much of her teaching – nuggets of distilled wisdom which are perhaps more important to us today than ever before in our desire to take the next step up in spiritual awareness.

When it came to giving a title to this book I was spoilt for choice, for Gladys herself had used three alternative titles: *Deep Twilight*, *Soliloquy of a Medium*, and *Ghosts Walk*! The one I have gone with is *Ghosts Walk*! and here is my reasoning.

Gladys uses the term *Deep Twilight* to refer to the

deep twilight of sleep, a half-waking state where one is partly asleep and so able to see upon a dimension other than that of the earth. It would have made a lovely title, except for the fact that it is not self-explanatory to the uninitiated reader.

Similarly, I can imagine a questioning eyebrow being raised at the title *Soliloquy of a Medium*. The word soliloquy means the action of speaking aloud to oneself. Therefore, though *Soliloquy of a Medium* hints at an invitation to listen in and share the inmost thoughts and feelings of the author, I feel it is not an obvious term that a newcomer to this field of enquiry would use when searching on the internet for a book giving answers to some of life's most profound questions.

That leaves *Ghosts Walk!* as my personal choice, certainly the most immediately relatable title. For Gladys did indeed see and hear what are commonly thought of as ghosts, or spirits, or discarnate individuals. I must emphasise that this was only the starting point of her investigations, which is why I have added the subtitle, *Autobiography of a Medium and Spiritual Teacher*. Again I must qualify these words, for Gladys was very much more than a medium. In addition, she always preferred the word 'natural' instead of 'spiritual', because the latter term has both religious and spiritualist overtones that are irrelevant to actually using the light of the soul, which is *natural* to life. Again, I could not expect the uninitiated to know this, so I have kept with the term 'spiritual teacher'.

These points aside, my real hope in publishing this autobiography of Gladys' extraordinary life, is that it will inspire its readers with the teaching that she so loved to be able to pass on to others, as well as providing a unique insight into the mind of an outstanding teacher and human being.

C. E. Jones – editor.

Gladys Franklin as a young woman

1. FACES AT THE WINDOW

Life for me has been full of surprises – not always good, but generally interesting, though sometimes causing me much fear. When I was a child I never knew when someone far removed from this earth might come face to face with me. I had no one to whom I could talk and no one I could rely upon for comfort. I tried to make a confidant of one of my brothers but giggles and pranks were the result and I was forced to hold my tongue.

People I had never seen before showed themselves to me, sometimes coming into my room, at other times peering at me through the window. When I tried to question them there were no encouraging words spoken out, only a nod, a smile, or perhaps a frown. Even their tentative smiles vanished quickly as fear flooded my mind. I did not then understand as I do now that discarnate individuals do not easily hear the spoken word, but words in the form of thought can be understood by them.

Truth of oneself is seen in colour, and many words are in the auric colours that surround each individual – the aura being the subconscious mind that stores much the brain does not readily take responsibility for. After reading the colours and seeing the truth of an individual, many unseen

1

observers quickly depart when not comfortable with what they see. Others who think the same way as the individual will keep near, encouraging him or her at times to develop awareness of their presence. My fear at that time would have made my thoughts muddled and unreadable, as they came from beneath the bedclothes under which I often took refuge.

No one made me aware of the power of the soul. No one told me how its light attracts like a magnet, drawing astrally bound people who expect some help in their release from the bondage of being invisible near the earth. Man is tentative in his seeking the unknown, his approach lacking power and the soul losing its life force, many feeling the result. Today, however, I do not fear in the same way, having learned in my sleep how to reach a point of conversation with people who have passed from the earth life and even those from outer space. Much I have learned, though yet there could be very much more.

For the first years of my life our family lived in a four-roomed flat with very little room for privacy. My mother and father worked hard to keep us clean and healthy, although sometimes my mother – overtired by all she had to do – took away our joy. I did not in those days know the great value of love. Had I found understanding, I may have known how to be of more help to her.

As children much of our play took place in

the street. I was tall for my age, and therefore the others tended to treat me as somewhat older, looking to me for ideas to keep them amused. I was determined to do something that might arouse interest. I found it easy to prop my small brother in his pram against the wall, giving me an opportunity to organise games. My parents began to wonder why there was no quarrelling amongst the children. I realise now that giving help to those other children encouraged the light to feed my soul. Sadly this ended when our family moved a distance away from that area, and I no longer found the same companionship and missed it greatly.

I was eight years old when we moved into a newly built council house with four bedrooms and an untold luxury – a bathroom! The house was comfortable and my parents happy with the exchange, but for a while the light of my soul went out. My joy came, however, when my mother allowed me a room at the front of the house, which I shared with my younger sister. I was elated, thinking myself to be free of the visitants that came without my invitation.

Another consolation I quickly discovered was that fields were all around us, even though much of our estate was still a building site with many houses partly erected. Flowers grew abundantly in those fields. Tall and stately buttercups and daisies swayed in the summer breeze like dancers dancing in a sea of tall grass, beautiful to behold and lovely to play in. I had never known before the sweet smell of new-mown hay, and all too short were the days that allowed us to romp in it and to bury each other whilst screaming with heady delight.

The farmers in those days did not fear that their property would be despoiled, and they generally did not prevent intrusion. The shrill cries of children tossing the hay amused more than irritated our local farmers and we were not driven away. We revelled in the freedom we found every day that was a holiday.

One winter's night I lay in my bed, alone in the darkness save for my sister who was fast asleep across the room. I had never liked the dark. To me it seemed to hold secrets that I was unable to share. At least this was so until that particular evening when, despite the blackness which enveloped everything, light appeared to be coming from outside my bedroom window. My eyelids fluttering, I became very frightened. For there looking at me through the window were three or more men dressed like pirates of many years before.

Each man wore a brightly striped jersey fitting tightly over his muscular body. On each head, knotted over the right ear, was a gaily coloured bandanna. Their faces, pressed against the window, showed knives between their teeth, the teeth so white that they appeared to sparkle in the light each one was giving off. The light gleaming about them was so bright that it spread throughout my room, so much so that I feared it might awaken my sister, who, mercifully, slept soundly through it all.

I remember quite clearly the one nearest to the window pane whose head shone in the light. His bright yellow bandanna was pulled low upon his forehead, completely covering his hair. The golden earring swinging from his left ear took on an additional glow that seemed to surround his face, enhancing the clear-cut lines of his features. Even with the knife between his teeth his expression was not menacing, his smile taking away any look of severity that may have been apparent.

I felt fear rise in me, affecting my breathing. Had I been able to leave my bed I would have fled to the bathroom. But nothing happened. The men made no attempt to come through the window, and for the first time during a visitation I did not slide down between the sheets. Every man was smiling. I began to feel almost a part of them and when I smiled too they became excited and waved their hands as, still laughing, they simply melted away.

2. A PAST INCARNATION SHOWS

My bedroom, small but cosy, was over the front porch and near to the top of the stairs. It was quite easy for me to hear the tread upon the stairs of anyone who came up (even if their step was light), because here and there the new wood squeaked.

One night when all was quiet I lay in my bed awake, quietly thinking and listening to my sister's gentle breathing, when a sound downstairs made me feel cold with fear. Someone had come into the house. My brothers had been upstairs for some time and my parents I had heard go into their room. I should have heard if anyone had gone downstairs for a drink. The noise increased. Surely my parents could hear, as I could myself. I tried to scream as heavy footsteps commenced to ascend the stairs. No one in the house stirred. I found I could not call out, the words jamming in my throat. Wildly I looked around, but there was nowhere to hide.

Before I could do anything to arouse my parents, the door slowly opened. A scream rose up within me, but only a sigh came from me as the door was pushed wider and two men entered my room dressed as Cavaliers. They did not look upon me with kindly eyes as the pirates had done. I took one look at their large feathered hats and dived down under the covers for refuge. The men were intent upon their mission, and only a few steps were needed to bring them to my bed. I heard the sound of steel being drawn from scabbards. I tried to make myself as small as I could, dreading what would come next. My visitors took no notice of the fear that I felt. Perhaps they were not aware of it, for they began to prod the bed with the point of their swords. I felt nothing however, and they made no effort to expose me.

At last they appeared satisfied with what they had done, for I heard the metallic swish as the swords were returned to their scabbards, and the click as they were made fast. They turned and went out of the room talking in loud voices, the sound of their heavy footsteps echoing in my ears as their boots thudded across the linoleum. They were soon going down the stairs as noisily as they had come up. I was amazed that no movement of my family was evident.

The sequel to this intrusion into my room came many years later when I was an established medium. The incident had been almost forgotten but was rudely brought back to me one night when, tired after a long day, I went to bed early. My sleep was strange; I appeared to be wide awake and yet knew I was asleep.

First of all I had risen from my bed in my inner body. I was floating around the room near the ceiling, looking down at my earth body upon the bed. I was totally unprepared for what came next, moving quickly towards the wall. I let out a scream as I met the solidity of the plaster and brick, but in seconds I was through, having felt no impact. The feeling was glorious as I went high in the air.

How I arrived at the castle I did not know. It was a dark and forbidding place but seemed to lighten as I went through an outside wall, moving swiftly down some steps that led deep underground into a dungeon. Suddenly I saw a girl who looked exactly like myself. She was about eighteen years of age, wearing a dress and apron with a round frilled cap upon her head. A young woman not much older than her, apparently sick, was lying on a mattress of straw upon a bench bed.

The door to the dungeon was not locked, but the girl made no attempt to get out. A man looking like a Quaker hurriedly came in. He took one look at the girl – my counterpart – and said, "Hot water. Hurry wench!" Looking on, I felt myself go into a trance-like state and could not move. I could only watch as the girl shrank away from him. The man was an apothecary. He was sharp-featured, and his tone matched his face. I saw the girl that was me pushed toward the stone steps of the stairway. She almost fell, so hard was the push. Seeing this I wanted to remonstrate, but the man could not hear me.

Suddenly and without warning I found myself climbing the stairway. No longer was I just watching the girl – I had now become that girl. Breathless, I came to a large kitchen. Hanging on the bare walls were pots and pans, burnished and gleaming oddly in the gloom of the place from where meals were served. I quickly asked for hot water and without any questions was given a large, steaming bowlful. Stumbling with the weight of the bowl, I went down the stairs, fearful of falling.

My mistress, the young woman upon the pallet, did not appear to know what was happening. I looked on helplessly. After muttering to himself, the apothecary turned to me and said, "She is asleep. Do not disturb her." I nodded and he went past me, quickly mounting the steps and moving out of my sight.

I looked at the bowl of water and thought, 'Not for me the terror of going all the way back to the kitchens. Someone will come with food. They can take the bowl back with them.' Thus ran my thoughts of self-protection.

A sound of voices above broke into my reverie. I tried to take no notice and began to lay the straw across the doorway where I was to sleep, the idea being that an intruder would find me first and my mistress would have warning. My master was a Cromwellian, a Roundhead, and my mistress – his daughter – and I had been hidden to keep us safe. The Master was away, and it was thought that enemies would not look for anyone other than him. In this they were wrong, for the voices I could hear came from Cavalier soldiers releasing their imprisoned men from the cells above. They were laughing uproariously at other prisoners who thought they also were going to escape.

I had finished laying down the straw, and having seen my mistress still asleep I was about to lie down myself, when soldiers appeared at the bend in the stairway. I had seen these men before, but at that time could not remember where. Speedily they reached me. As the men took hold of my arms I almost fell, only to find a rope being looped round my neck. As I screamed the rope was pulled tighter, and laughter sounded in my ears as I began to lose consciousness. My mistress had been awakened and was bewildered at men pulling her from her uncomfortable couch. I knew then that her fate was sealed. The next moment I found myself back in my own bed, the experience over. Hurriedly I went for a drink of water, my throat feeling very dry.

I know from all I have learned over many years, that education for one's life can be received when one is out of the earth body, including the showing of past incarnations. This whole experience was repeated three times over three nights before I spoke up loudly saying, "All right, do not give me this again! I will believe in reincarnation."

A further sequel came some years later. I was taken in a dream to a large house. People were being introduced to a man whose bearing was soldierly. This was the Duke of Marlborough, a renowned military leader of the period of time I was then visiting – some years after the end of the civil war between Cavaliers and Roundheads. He held out his hand to me as my companion introduced us. As we shook hands he said, "My men have been over-zealous; they have troubled you. Please forgive us – not all soldiers know when wars in the earth have come to an end!"

3. A PREHISTORIC MONSTER

I was intrigued by all these things and wanted to know more of things historical. Since then I have experienced many living tableaux of the past. There was even a night when I was taken to meet Michelangelo, for whom I'd long had great admiration. At the time it gave me much food for thought, for although his personality was as expected, his clothes resembled those of modern times. He was, I remember, very busy at the time, being somewhat ambushed by people. He shook hands with me, but apart from thanking me for admiring his work he said nothing. Brief as the encounter was, it is something that I treasure to this day.

But now I am jumping ahead of myself in the telling of my life. I must return to my early years, when there were many nights I ran away just before bedtime. Facing the displeasure of my mother was nothing to the fear I felt when having unwanted visitors. I could not tell my parents as they were very down-to-earth people. Their days were long and arduous and I did not wish them to laugh at me as they certainly would have done had I disclosed my fears.

Although I have spoken mainly of unwanted visitors, there were at times, over a number of years, various visitors I was quite happy to see. Not always was anything said, but invariably assurance was given such that it caused me to wonder greatly of what was in store for me. It was in this manner that I first saw Crusader. He was always accompanied by his white horse. It thrilled me to see him, for he was courteous and kind. The lovely trappings upon the body of the horse were brilliant in colour. I sigh even now when I think of Crusader's gentle approach, so contrary to the men of the Cavalier times, though they may have appeared to be romantic.

Though I did not understand it then, I was gradually being made aware that the night-time brought a sequel to much that happened during the day. There were times when I thrilled to scenes I could never at any time witness on the earth.

Time passed by and life became more exacting than it had been previously. The General Strike of 1926 hit many jobs up and down the country. I was working some miles from my home and found it ironic that travelling to and from work was easier for me through this time of disruption than at other times. Normally I had at least two miles to walk, both in the morning and in the evening after a long day on my feet. But the problems brought on by the strike somehow made people more considerate, as often happens in times of trouble, and I found that each morning and evening saw a different car stopping at the kerb and the driver offering me a lift. This was a new and joyous experience for me, for I had never ridden in a car before that time. Travelling in this way, the distance to and from work seemed nothing at all. I was exceedingly glad to be able to feel fresh on arrival at my job. The day could not pass quickly enough for me, knowing that I would arrive home much earlier and have more free time in the evening.

One night I went to a dance. My mother, anxious for me, had said, "Ten o'clock and no later." This gave me two hours to enjoy before having to run to get home on the dot of ten o'clock, arriving home breathless and being quickly ushered off to bed.

I soon fell asleep, and suddenly I was dreaming that I was walking hurriedly along the main street, which was called 'The Broadway'. The shops were shut and no one was about. I began to feel afraid, which was nothing new to me in the state of sleep. The experience appeared as real as if I were wide awake, and I gazed longingly in a shop in which hung a beautiful dress. It was at that precise moment that violent screams rent the air. I turned from the shop, ready to run. Looking one way I saw only the peaceful main road. Turning to look in the other direction, however, I was hypnotised with shock and for a moment could not move, for a great prehistoric monster was lumbering down the centre of the road.

The creature almost filled the road as it took

great strides. Its tail slashed the shops, bringing down the flats that were above them. Blood was dripping from its great jaws as its teeth clamped upon one and then another of the people as they fell to the ground within the rubble of their houses. Helpless, they quickly died, along with many others I watched that never had a chance. I decided to move and ran speedily to the next turn in the road, which would bring me near to home. I seemed to know instinctively that the creature was striking only the places of business.

This same scene I see every time there is going to be a strike. I was at that time looking through the eyes of loving people who were helping me to learn of life. I do not remember reaching my home in that dream, but woke up to the realisation I had been watching the effects of an all-out strike originally intended only to bring benefit. I remember thinking wildly, 'Why does God allow this to happen?'

Being seventeen at the time, I was old enough to realise that insufficient wages were causing much hardship, especially in the winter months. My father and elder brother were both working on the railway; their wages were very poor and looked as though they might stay that way if nothing was done about it. I strongly felt that it was terrible how something supposed to help men like my father and brother could instead give rise to devastation, affecting so many businesses and those who relied upon them for their livelihood.

As I lay awake, I could remember turning round in the dream and seeing smoke and flames rising up to the night sky, the beauty of which was so savagely torn by the great beast ambling along, its head and tail doing more damage than any bomb might have done. I could visualise the scene, the place like a battlefield where two sides – the businesses and the workers – had fought but where little more than enmity, resentment and distrust would be gained. Nothing was left standing. It became evident to me that many more than those who struggled for a rise in pay would suffer, for the strike had already been going on for a few days, and more than a few businesses, to a large extent helpless against the actions of the strikers, were finding themselves in dire straits.

I pondered upon what I had seen, holding it to myself, feeling that no one would believe me. I was to realise later that I had seen something of great import, but at the time I did not fully understand the significance of it all. When my father and brother were brought out on strike with all the other railwaymen, however, I took in the lesson and found the truth of it, for it started a landslide of almost everything connected with daily life. Money became almost nil. My mother found work as a daily housekeeper and a cook in a large pub, which amazingly did very well despite the rigour of many lives. But the work was heavy; her health had not been good and she found great difficulty in carrying on.

Shops could obtain no new stock, and though the strike was not prolonged it was long enough to kill new businesses. Even some old-established firms lost ground and began to fall. Hardship was the lot of many, and who can say what tragedies were enacted in the homes of proprietors and workers alike.

I became very quiet. I feel I grew up at that time, my mind full of the difficulties being endured. One cannot run away from these things but I tried by going swimming and dancing. I lost the dreams I had become used to having, and although I missed them I put no real value upon them.

Few people knew there could be another approach to settling a strike. At that time I was unaware of the importance of prayer, but I found it beginning to come easily for me. Like many other people, I prayed that God would remove the man-made burdens that were despoiling much that hard work had built up. I knew, however, that people had to play their part, and it was some years later that I really recognised the truth of this. Previously, God had been to me like a loving father. On understanding cause and effect, I had to think in wider terms than seeing God as a man in heaven, and by the aid of meditation I began to visit planes of life that previously I never knew existed.

4. FOREVER SEEKING

As I reached and passed my teenage years I found myself seeking, looking for something I could not find. My inner self was never very content. It always seemed to want to be elsewhere as if looking for someone or something. I never associated this with the visitors I had seen in my earlier years, thinking as many young women do of the love of a home and the children that might come. We seek in many ways, sometimes not understanding that the first steps towards our seeking are simply homely ones that teach us to love other people more than ourselves.

My seeking mind had not taught me a great deal. I thought much the same as other young people, loving to sing and dance. I joined a society that put on shows for the aged. I enjoyed every moment of the rehearsals and the performances, which often turned out to be quite hilarious. I have since felt that these shows prepared me for facing the public. The experience laid a foundation which may not have been found in any other way. It was through these activities that I was to meet my husband.

My father and brothers belonged to the Brotherhood of Hendon, which I subsequently joined. They were in the male voice choir which was well noted in Hendon. My membership helped me to overcome my nervous disposition while playing the violin and forgetting myself. The very popular Sunday afternoons, when the Brotherhood met, were always enjoyed. The hall we used was on the main road, but the clank of the trams did not disturb the air of upliftment that everyone looked forward to feeling.

My parents insisted that we all went to church. We firstly attended the High Church, St John's, where we did not feel very comfortable. Later we went to the Baptist Church in Hendon, where a very good pastor blessed his flock with loving consideration. All this time, dreams, visions and experiences in all kinds of circumstances were given to me. Sometimes these elated me. At other times however, they depressed me.

My years of tuition toward the project (The Project of the Golden Ball, explained later) were unknown to me when, at the age of twenty-one, I was married in Hendon Baptist Church. My first baby was a girl. Her early years were a trial as she did not eat very well. However, after an operation at the age of three, she thrived and became very sturdy. She has been both a daughter and a friend to me.

My second child was a boy, and I nearly lost him because he was born two months premature. Being only a seven-month-old baby he was just like a doll, and everyone watched his growth with nervous anticipation. The loving care he received at the hospital, however, enabled him to grow to full size. Care of him took all my time and I had to give up my Sunday activities with the Brotherhood of Hendon. When my third child was born I gave up my music, filling my time with the making of clothes for the whole family.

In having to give up the rest of my activities for a while, I became sad and felt very keenly the need for companionship. This inward need seemed to impose itself on my sleepstates (dreams), and on one occasion whilst taking a rest on a Saturday afternoon, I was roused from sleep to find a form bending over me. Seeing a Native American with full feathered headdress made me gasp in astonishment, which brought a smile to his face.

The feathers were pale mauve tipped with white and as he leaned over me they fell forward, framing his face and mine. I just had to tell him how beautiful he was! The light flowing from him outshone the brilliant sunshine which was also flooding the room. I lay there for about five minutes taking in the living features before he faded away. His visit seemed to open up a corner of my brain, because I began to write stories. My children were my greatest literary critics, never failing to tell me if they thought that a story was not very good.

My knowledge of Spiritualism until that time, my twenty-seventh year, was very little. However, I began to learn more when my youngest sister had a number of sties on her eyelids. These were very painful and her health deteriorated. The doctor, who was most considerate, seemed unable to help apart from suggesting a tonic. My mother, not knowing what to do but having been told of meetings held in a hall over the local cinema, wondered if it was worth taking my sister along to see if her condition could be alleviated. Mr Daisley, a truly wonderful medium, was on the platform when my mother finally made up her mind to go.

When the meeting was over, Mr Daisley did not ask for my sister to be brought for healing. Instead, he simply put his hands on her eyes and said, "Tomorrow they will be quite all right. She will never have sties again." His words have been proven correct over the years. Although ill health has struck hard at times, the painful eyes have never returned.

My mother encouraged me to go to the next meeting that Mr Daisley was taking. He really held the attention of everyone, all admiring his skill as a medium. Working from the platform, he told the men all they had in their pockets. He confounded everyone more by being able to tell the women the contents of their handbags, and on emptying them into their laps all that he had said was confirmed. He could even tell them just how much they had in their purse! Such mediumship was my target for many years of my development. However, I have had to tread a different path which, though hard at times, I would never want to change.

When we were about to leave the hall my mother whispered to me, "Isn't he wonderful?"

Without thinking I replied, "Yes, he is, but I could do that."

"Vanity will get you nowhere," she said, emphasising her words. Then she added, "I will take you where you will prove your words, my girl."

What prompted me to speak as I did? I had no intention of saying anything to push myself forward. However, I had to follow my mother as she promptly made for a lady who was surrounded by a number of people. She was Mrs Rosa Parvin, a famous psychic artist of that time. Her pictures were truly works of art and her personality was well above average.

After a few minutes my mother directed me to stand in front of her, pointing out to the medium what I had just said. Rosa laughed, and putting me at my ease said, "Well, perhaps she can. Bring her along to our next circle night."

She told my mother the address, the day and the date regarding the circle. We thanked Mrs Parvin, and my mother walked away with a very satisfied air. I followed somewhat meekly, though I must admit that I was hugging to myself the secret I had carried for so many years of which my parents knew nothing.

The day came and worry set my nerves jangling, but we were not long in Mrs Parvin's company before I felt the quietness and peace of that room.

Prayer was said and all were quiet as meditation began. Within minutes I was back in time, delighted to be sitting on a high wall and watching an attack upon a castle.

As I sat, I described clothing, weapons and the way the fight was going. Listening to the shouts of the soldiers and the screams of the wounded, all was so realistic that it seemed as though I was really there. For twenty minutes I watched, speaking all the time and keeping every listener interested. I was very disappointed when silk curtains fell in front of me. Only then was I able to open my eyes and take note of the intent expression on the face of each sitter.

Rosa Parvin was very pleased and assured my mother that I did have something. This was very clearly the case, but the silk curtains meant that I had to work to bring out that which was there. We were told that this might take a little time.

My husband was not in total agreement with my seeking, but he did not stop me from going anywhere I wished. However, I had very little money as he had been out of work for some time, and so Mrs Parvin's invitation to join their group was sadly turned down. Having no one to encourage me I did not do very much about my development.

The family took up much of my time, but we went again and again to hear the wonderful speakers and demonstrators whose pioneering days were often looked down upon by the general public. The hall we went to had a seating capacity of around two hundred and was always full of very expectant people.

I heard Mr Daisley many times at that place. Another favourite medium was Mr John Lovatt. His quiet confidence in the love of the Spirit laid a foundation for myself which has blessed me many times. It has also helped me to maintain quietness – even under persecution.

5. TUITION FOR A TEACHER

At the time of my meeting with Michelangelo my daily life increased its burden. My husband fell ill, and it was an illness that was to last a very long time. Earning for my family was not at all easy and it was difficult to see how I would cope. I learned patience by standing in a queue waiting for coupons for bread and meat for my children. Tolerance did not come easily, for people mocked those who stood waiting for charity, and when taking the coupons to the shop I was given only stale bread in exchange and meat not wanted by other people. Children today have no knowledge of the hard knocks some had to take, but I learned.

Help came in unexpected ways, however, but only in times of real need. Pound notes would drop in front of me if I could not afford food, and gifts put upon the doorstep aided my resolve to keep giving time to my learning and development, which in turn would be used to help others.

My landlady on one occasion allowed me to be relieved of paying rent. My heart went out to her as she said, "Accept that as help towards your son's education." What blessings one can receive, as I learned more each day. I truly have proven that giving full thought to the blessing of other people ensures that one's own wisdom is increased. Freely one gives of mind and time, and freely will one receive.

During this time, although I was still not fully developed, I settled down to learning and to helping anyone I could. I prayed long and earnestly and was given the advice to start a place of healing and the giving of comfort to the needy. I found much blessing in healing animals as well as people, and I rejoiced to find people coming from many miles away and not needing to come a second time. This gave me great confidence and carried me along, and after 1939 when the war commenced I was able to help RAF airmen during the weeks of the Battle of Britain.

Becoming exhausted through long periods of flying without sufficient rest meant there was no protection around them. It allowed unhelpful spirits to cling to them and to interfere with their brain, so much so that they would not go home on leave because of not wanting to take with them the unhappiness they had been made to feel. I noticed when treating some of them that a dark green vapour would come out of the stomach forming into a head. It showed the possessing spirit being forced to leave, unable to stand the light.

The airmen, having been imbued with added life force, were happy to go straight home to those they loved. I myself felt blessed at being instrumental in helping them, love being the key that pride must never be allowed to kill.

Sitting in bed one evening reading my Bible, I came across the words, that the greatest gift one can have is teaching, and said aloud, "If that's the greatest, that's for me!" If vanity was the motivation for my spontaneous choice, I have since learned much to wipe this from my consciousness, having been humbled many times.

I was not to know at that time what repercussions were to come from that passage, for I was not aware of the importance of the spirit body and its seeking – the free will of which is constantly urging its way. It needs the cooperation of the brain for the spirit self to organise the way ahead for the matter self. Teaching comes accordingly, no matter how one may wish to change the brain afterwards.

Some weeks went by during which I had various visitations from spirits, who, having introduced themselves and spoken of the work that was to be done, went their way. I thought little about their words or indeed of those that had come from me, until I was jolted out of my lethargy by another experience.

Leaving the body had by then become so natural to me, that at any time when relaxing I found myself outside the earth body and its limitations. Enjoyment of food was not part of my daily life, but in the spirit world I was able to eat all the foods I liked without irritation to my digestion. From the daytime the night became apparent, and I found I could get an answer to my thoughts just by sending them out and waiting. However, when emotional thoughts were heavy on me I could not find my way to light and happiness, and the answers to my queries were invariably untrue, showing me that only truth coming from oneself can anticipate truth in reply. After absorbing this point, I was once again taken for a further experience which was to alter my whole life.

About that time I was receiving many dreams concerning everyday life, the valuable experience of which will always alter seemingly solid barriers, because it sets new causes in motion. My physical self had stated that I wanted to teach; my spirit self had set this going, so the two parts of me were in harmony. But what of the astral self, which duly takes its cue from the subconscious mind? This contrary part of one often offends, by altering the course one would like to take. Its ready knowledge of frets, fears and fallacies, cutting down the positive mind and bringing in a negative outlook, is not always understood for what it is, and blame, rarely seeming to lie with oneself, is often left at someone else's door.

Looking back, it appears that that particular night had been chosen, for immediately my head touched the pillow the bed was no longer there. I was walking along a road, deep in conversation with a very pleasant gentleman. He talked fluently and well, but gave no indication of what was about to happen. My release from the earth body had been quite different from that of previous occasions. There was no thrilling sensation, but an instant release from one body to the other, almost as if the same body was being used. In fact, there seemed no difference at all; I was wearing the same clothes, and was even conscious that I had been hot when serving a church earlier in the day, and that my clothes were not entirely fresh. Apart from this I enjoyed the walk very much, and the intelligent conversation too. There seemed to be little exertion needed, and although I had been very tired I did not feel it now. Instead, I felt alive, exhilarated, and was really glad of a walk in the country, being somewhat tied at home.

All too soon we came to a house, with spacious lawns and lovely flowerbeds. It was beautiful to look at, and I wondered whom we were going to see. My companion pulled on an ornate bell and almost at once a trim maid opened the door. She looked at me in a startled manner, but recovered and asked us in. She seemed to know the man with me, whose identity I never found out. Walking upstairs I noticed an air of peace about the whole place. The thick carpet and hushed steps added to this sense of peace, and I sighed as my mind went to the trials of my own life. But a shock awaited me.

Arriving at the bedroom door my companion knocked, and a voice bid us enter. The room was everything of which I had ever dreamed, but my eyes were drawn to the sumptuous bed in which sat a woman, surrounded by pillows. A small dog was warmly cuddled in the crook of her arm.

Before we had time to speak, there was a soft tap on the door; the maid came in, and very discreetly placed a breakfast tray on the bed. In a small vase was a posy of flowers, which seemed to add a glow to the daintily-arranged food. Another deep sigh escaped me, but even as it left my lips I saw that the woman in bed was myself. My mind went quickly to precognition. Was this going to be my house and was this life going to be mine? The prospect should have filled me with joy, but instead I felt repelled, and turning to my companion, said, "But this isn't what I want. I want to be a teacher."

Smiling, he said, "Are you sure? All this can be yours. You are the one that must choose. The way of a teacher is hard, and there will be many things to suffer in order that you will see everything exactly as it is. You will not always have light, for you must seek in darkened places so as to know life as it really is."

The more he went on in this vein, the less I wanted to change my mind.

"The subconscious mind must learn to hold truth all the time," he continued, "so you must face up to the teaching and let the past go. All these things are a natural procedure, for all is of life and nothing must be left out. You will glimpse many things and learn from them. The rest is up to you. People will come and go; some will learn and others will deride, but have no fear, for as you learn so you will come to terms with life."

6. SING FOO

From that night onwards I continued to have experiences, mostly when asleep or just upon waking. These experiences came as a natural effect from causes set going during the day. I had a great deal to do, for the responsibility of the home fell on my shoulders, but by getting up very early in the morning was able to leave two hours in the afternoon for meditation and tuition.

I was no longer fearful as I had been in my earlier life. This of course was a great help to me in my investigations, because I could look into things with the confidence that is so necessary when one wishes to find truth. The desire to seek is of little use if one is too afraid to take the steps to learn. I was understandably very grateful that fear no longer held me back in this respect and I could now seek in a way which was to give me priceless experience and understanding.

My work towards a fuller understanding of the Spirit had so far been like exploring without a map. I was somewhat like a child at school, having all the books available from which to learn, but not knowing how to make the best of my opportunities. I had no teacher to help me choose my course of study, but this situation was soon to change.

One Saturday, when the children had gone to play in the park, I was alone in the house. My husband was with my father and brothers who were playing cricket in an away game to which I was unable to go. Hurrying to get everything cleared up, I finished early and went to my bedroom to rest.

I found myself on the way to the train station. The walk was decidedly hazardous, for I had to watch out for large stones that seemed to just pop up and become set fast in the road. So often had I covered space by swift flight through the air, that at first my mind wandered in an effort to find out why an orthodox method of transport was being taken.

Arriving somewhat breathlessly at the station, I hurried to the ticket office, only to be thwarted again by the inability to get a ticket. The man looked at me unseeingly, and as the minutes passed I tried to attract his attention, but without success.

Hastily I left the ticket office as the train came hurtling into the station. It has always been an excitement to me to ride in a train, more especially in those days of steam. Yet there was no smoke to be seen, which rather intrigued me. I have since found out that the spirit world has no coal industry, and movement – whether fast or slow – is far more to do with mind.

All was bustle and confusion until everyone was on board. It was only when I was sitting down that I realised I had no idea where I was heading. The train was obviously going some distance before its next stop, so I began fretting a little.

But the scenery was lovely, and as I feasted my eyes on it my fears dissolved away, and I sat back to enjoy the ride. I knew I was safe and could rely on the train taking me somewhere. The more I thought about it the less I wondered about the destination, and at last filled myself completely with the pleasure of the journey. It seems somewhat stupid to say that I awoke even as the train roared on, to find myself in the quiet of my own room.

It was still daylight. I lay on my back, pondering on the unfinished journey I had just taken. My attention was caught by the colours that were coming and going over the high ceiling. Bright and beautiful they surged, completely changing from one lovely hue to another. The pattern the colours followed was circular in movement, swirling from the centre to the outside of the room, then changing colour two or three times before meeting back in the centre to form one huge, exquisitely beautiful flower. This had often happened before whenever I lay quietly, but this time the colours were stronger than I had previously known. The whole ceiling was radiating brightness with great bars of colour spread across it.

Spellbound, I watched with wide open eyes as a pair of large feet came through the ceiling in the middle of the brightest patch of colour.

Intrigued, I watched the feet slowly descend. The time seemed interminable. Gradually the feet were followed by long legs covered by a soft gown that flowed about them. I thought at first that the body would never come, but slowly it materialised. The movement was graceful and unhurried, and then at last the lovely smiling face of a Chinese gentleman appeared looking down at me.

When at last he stood on the floor I could see he was quite seven foot tall, and wore a simple hat of a style that we associate with Mandarins. He was clean and bright in his white robe, which was loosely caught up around the waist. His hands were long and shapely, and a light surrounded him as he moved. I could see right through him and yet his figure was perfect. I was too excited to be afraid.

My mind tumbled over itself. Who was it? Would it be someone I knew? It was most certainly a discarnate being, and one not used to putting in an appearance.

Coming to the foot of the bed, his whole being giving me encouragement, he began to speak. "My name is Sing Foo," he said, his voice quiet but easy to hear. Confidence flowed from him into me as he spoke. I became more and more elated.

"You will hear a great deal of me," he continued, watching my reaction. I was stunned, neither moving nor speaking.

His English was quite understandable and his voice had a soft, pleasant timbre. At first I did not take in his words, so stupefied was I by his presence. But then he began to repeat urgently what he had been saying.

Suddenly I knew that if I did not grasp the message I would lose its portent, and I began to concentrate so as not to miss a word. As he continued quietly talking I grew more and more excited, for he was a teacher, and I was going to be taught to be one such myself. Having wanted this for some time, I was delighted to find the first positive step being taken. Now a vision was put in front of me; a vast open space, with few trees to give shelter. The earth was rough and full of troughs, as it had been deeply ploughed. I could see myself stumbling over the uneven ground, my feet heavy with mud, and my head bowed against the driving wind.

Much deflated, I looked in dismay at my visitor. "Do you still want to go on with it?" he asked.

Laughing at my jitters, I said, "Yes of course. It can't be as hard as it looks."

"It might be more so," he replied, "for you can worsen it and make life hard in the extreme. But if you learn well, you will be allowed to see beyond the dismal picture you have just seen. You must start being more reliant on your own inner impetus. This is the symbol of the train; you can be carried from one circumstance to another, and from one place to another, if you rely more upon your inner body and less on your outer. There are many stones upon which you could hurt yourself, but if you watch the way carefully and hold peace within yourself, nothing will be too heavy to bear. The outcome of the journey of life will be as you have made it. You can teach many, if you have the courage to learn."

Sobered by his grave words, I asked him if in some way his visit could be confirmed. For it all seemed far beyond my comprehension, and I wanted more than anything else to do good in the world.

"Tomorrow you will hear of me." And with these words fading away, he nodded farewell and just disappeared.

In wonderment at what I had seen, I sat in bed, nonplussed and rather light-headed. I did not want to move, but the day began to make its demands, and before very long I was immersed in meeting my family's needs.

7. A CONFIRMATION

The next day was a Sunday morning. Like one sleepwalking I went through the chores that had to be done, hoping to be free later to visit the small local church in Church End, Hendon – a bus ride from my home. Inwardly I was seething with excitement, agog to see if other people there had shared my experience in some way. Just then a number of my family arrived, and being a very happy crowd I found it difficult to leave until they had settled down to a game of cards. This was a game that I myself never played, because my undeveloped psychic faculties caused me to see kings, queens and jacks walking about my room.

I was late arriving at the church. The service was well under way but I was not denied entry. To my great joy, the medium in spite of my late arrival came firstly to me.

"I see a very tall Chinese gentleman with you," she said. "He tells me that his name is Sing Foo. He is going to work with you and wants me to say that you are going to hear a lot from him."

I was almost dumb with happiness and could only stutter my thanks. The medium moved on to the next person, perhaps not knowing just what she had done for me. I now knew that I was on the way to progression and perhaps mediumship in the way I had hoped to know it.

After the meeting nobody seemed interested in what I had to say about the experience leading up to my message. I had met the first stone! It seemed to mean I could be slighted, and either hurt myself or throw it off with a smile. Inwardly I thanked my new friend for having prepared me. My joy was full, and never would I go back on my word, but I did not know of the harassing times ahead that would almost break me as I struggled to stick to my resolve.

I walked home on air that night, and I hope the medium was richly blessed, for I certainly showered thoughts of love upon her. I know now that when such blessing is being given, and appreciation full within one, the receiver can find everything in life rising. The knowledge of this fact has taught me never to stint appreciation, for its very presence means a wonderful uplift and blessing, both to the giver and the recipient.

I quite expected to see Sing Foo again or at least hear his voice, but I had no such pleasure. The effects of his work in the background could be seen in small, subtle ways. One example of this may sound rather silly, but it was of great importance to my education. Each morning when I awoke, I saw a thread of white light which looked like a piece of cotton on the door of the wardrobe at the side of my bed. I soon became used to seeing it and noticed that on some days the thread pointed upwards and on other days it pointed downwards. Sometimes it was V-shaped, pointing either upwards or downwards with the trailing ends coming from it.

I found that a very happy day would follow if the thread was pointing upwards, but some disturbing factor or other would have to be tackled if it was pointing downwards. I understood the trailing ends to mean that certain conditions would have to be cleared up, so this was a means of putting me on my guard.

I became very accustomed to getting depressed at seeing the thread going down or happy when seeing it going up. This subtle form of tuition went on until I realised that I became depressed for no reason at all and happy when the days were unproductive. At last I took myself to task, realising that a lesson had to be learned. There was no reason to go up or down. I should remain as happy and contented as I could, and do the best possible in order to gain the greatest help in whatever had to be done.

After learning this important lesson I was told that if I did not rise and fall, but could be trusted to keep agreeably minded, I could be given work that required an even mind. I was told in sleep that the Masters in Spirit cannot entrust work to those who allow emotions to sway the mind and so spoil any plans that are put into operation for further progress.

During my period of tuition under Sing Foo I had

taken up the work of a rostrum medium, going to varying churches to take services. I sat in certain circles but found them to be of very little help compared to what I could get from my own dreams and visions. As these became stronger I began to take notice of cause and effect, which they showed clearly. The children were growing older and they too began to have visions, and when having dreams we did all that we could to find the explanations to them.

I also commenced running meetings in my house in London. These, however, did not seem to be very successful. I know this was because I had much to learn, but in early days one does not always see the tuition that is so necessary for one who wishes to build up a centre or church. It took a while for me to realise that I was not in full harmony with myself. This caused ill health which, combined with the effects of World War II upon services and travel, made me give up any outside work.

Mediumship still took up much of my time, for I had many coming for consolation and help because of lost or missing loved ones. Friends and relatives of soldiers in prisoner-of-war camps brought cufflinks and ties to use as a mind link, by which means I was able to receive thought messages on their behalf. I found this work particularly rewarding and was able to learn much from it that was of great value to me.

8. THE COURTROOM

There was a time when I thought spirits could do everything; they had only to be asked. This notion was quickly dispelled by my discarnate teacher, Sing Foo. He was to take me through several years of tuition whilst yet allowing me to use my own will to prove things for myself. He made me see the many mistakes I made and I found that a lesson learned was a blessing gained, and as one lives so one has the possibility of learning.

Determination plays a very important part in life, both good and evil being served by it. As one thinks of one's own interests, the subconscious mind widens upon it to create circumstances accordingly, not always bringing the desired result. Proof of this was of considerable educational value to me, and was also a positive guide in life thereafter.

Once again sleep provided tuition, and gladly I accepted the lesson offered, although at first I had been inclined to rebel against earthly circumstances. In fact, it was this that brought about the unforgettable experience.

At that time, despite being able to help others, my own life was extremely burdensome. I was being increasingly harassed by people on the earth and subsequently in the spirit world too. Many wished to secure my services as a medium, but my own living conditions were not at all helpful to the work involved, and moreover, financial matters weighed heavily.

Deep down I felt disillusioned, sure that somewhere along the line I was being misled. Complaining to oneself amounts to letting the brain move against the inner self and making no attempt to stop it. I had not seen my helper spirit for some time, but felt sure that all I was thinking would be known to him. I knew that I was being left open to natural causes, but far more than seemed natural was pressing me down.

Thus the questioning brain, one's critical faculty, would not be stilled. Wishful thinking began to play a very large part in my life, as thoughts played hide-and-seek with me. At that time I did not know that wishful thinking could lead me into danger, but having learned that this is possible, I now watch the basic thought pattern which seeks to create circumstances in life.

When I fell asleep that night I was hoping to find myself in uplifting conditions, but this was not to be. A lesson had to be learnt, and protecting me would not have permitted tuition to take effect.

At first the place arrived at did not bother me, for I was just sitting and watching what was going on, but suddenly I realised that words were being said which shook my equanimity and set me pondering on why I was there. I was in a courtroom very like a court of law on earth. Gowned and bewigged figures were moving into place, judge, jury and lawyers kept busy as case after case was brought before them. I was amazed to find that everyone felt they were being misused and were feeling rather like myself – that spirits should relieve one's oppressive circumstances.

It was interesting to note that few were allowed added help, because much was proved to have been their own fault, brought upon themselves by their own words or actions. No one else had made life hard, and having accepted certain responsibilities it was not easy to drop them, until given an opportunity by the actual circumstances being eliminated. There were people who wanted to be divorced, and some were able to be freed from each other, while others were given various times when it might be possible to apply again. From this I understood that when there were valid grounds, a divorce obtained out of the body would secure it without incident on earth.

It was very much borne in upon me that everyone sees truth in his or her own way. We see through an emotional facade that completely blinds us to the real truth, but when emotions are stripped from the self, the truth emerges, clearly separated from the dross that was covering it. The plane of life reached during sleep will present the unvarnished truth for the subconscious mind to realise.

It seemed a very long time, just sitting and listening, but in becoming so interested I had almost forgotten the reason I was there. When at last my name was called, preliminaries had to be gone through and the oath had to be taken. I stood somewhat tremulously while something was confided to the judge; so quietly was it said that I could not catch it, but the judge looked up quickly and eyed me with something like suspicion. Just then, in one part of the court (equivalent to the public gallery, I suppose) a group of people had recognised me; people with whom I had become unpopular on earth. One of them shouted unpleasantly, "She has no business being here!" I wondered at this show of resentment, for I bore him no ill will. Gradually it sunk in that things were not going too well for me. Just when I began to think I had made a mistake in lodging a complaint, I was given an opportunity to state my case.

I made no mention of my teacher, Sing Foo, who had spoken to me about the positive work that was to be done. I just pointed out that I was disturbed about the bad feeling being caused by the spread of gossip.

Suddenly I saw Sing Foo being ushered into the court. He seemed loath to speak, and disinclined to answer the questions put to him. One fact he made very plain when he said, "She doesn't know very much, as she's not been studying the natural laws for very long."

There were shouts and boos directed at his evidence, and the judge had to call order. Sing Foo took little notice; his smile was encouraging, and I began to feel very small. I was called upon to state my precise objections to life. Somehow, with my teacher smiling at me, I could not find much to complain about, except the wagging tongues that were destroying everything I was trying to do.

My teacher was called on to answer my complaint, and he explained that effect had to be seen in a natural way, as part of my tuition. I had not been prepared for this, otherwise the outcome would have been different. Much was being researched about cause and effect that would help many people later on, if they wished to learn. At this there were more vocal protests, those who did not wish to learn showing their rebellious feelings.

Each of these people spoke piously on earth. They spoke of God as their own private property, but now they were shown for what they really were; a danger to the work and also to me. Sing Foo continued by saying he regretted that I had felt the need to come here. He had tried to show me the necessity of holding courage, warning me that the way would be hard. He added, which gratified me to learn, that when familiar spirits saw a sincere individual open themselves to research and study of the fuller life, they were liable to pursue a point of persuasion, and so make the way harder than it need be.

The judge had to intervene again as voices were raised in anger at what was said. "The court will be cleared if I have to speak again," he declared.

I was surprised that my teacher had no more to say, not even some comment on or explanation of the conduct of the onlookers in the courtroom. He sat quietly smiling, without further comment. I felt that surely people should know that he and others like him were fighting for the peace of the world.

Just then a young man got up. I had only seen his back, and the timbre of his voice as he spoke was particularly pleasing to the ear. "I will give her help," he said.

My teacher nodded his head as if quite satisfied with the outcome. The judge said, "Case dismissed!" And speaking directly at me, he added, "You should not have come to this court. We cannot interfere with the work of research tutors."

I was nonplussed, but before I could ask any questions my hand was strongly grasped, and almost pulling me off my feet was a man whose loincloth and turban showed definite signs of wear.

"Come!" he said as he ran with me, "We'll have to get away. I must show you the way back before anyone realises you're here, for those who hate the light would be glad to see you dead. They cannot bear the light because you show up the darkness around them. This is why they harass and persecute. Be strong, for I may not be on hand should you go another time to such a place.

I did not mind his tone of voice, he feared for me. To some extent I felt as if no one wanted to know my point of view, but it had not all been a waste of time. Subsequent events were to show that much had been learned, and knowledge, especially of life, was very valuable. It stood out in my mind that help had been offered, and what a blessing that would be if it could be manifested on earth.

When I was fully awake my brain began a busy round of nonsensical musings, until I was sharply pulled up by a voice speaking urgently. My brain, I was told, must be kept still, this being the only way that strength of character could be gained and everything necessary to life learnt.

The subconscious mind must discern and use determination to school the brain, so that everything within it needing alteration can be given attention. The brain, it was explained, can be of wonderful help when subject to the spirit self's wider understanding, but it can also be a hindrance if confused by supposition or other people's opinions. At that time I had scant knowledge on this point, and had not proved it to my own satisfaction.

Since then, knowledge has increased and its help has been beyond anything previously learned. I now understand karma as being the influence of the spirit self upon the mind. Once the brain allows the mind freedom to show the way, karma proves its value in visions and dreams. It has been proved that certain dreams can be brought into being by brain activity, unfortunately agitated and enlarged by uneducated discarnate individuals. Under such conditions karma is rarely present but is waylaid, while the subconscious reacts to the brain and its subsequent round of thought.

Thought creations bring action either in the right or the wrong way. By using the spirit self's initiative, karma is used, the mind subjecting the brain. In opposition to this, the brain can encourage progression of the earth, which does not always express the use of karma or give added opportunity to it. I have found it most disturbing to stave off karma by following the more popular directives of the brain, for although it brought material goods to me, it put my spirit self to sleep, whereupon I had to rely on spirits to work with me. It was therefore a joyful day when I found the spirit self reawakened and able to work once more.

I was a practising medium, perhaps too outspoken for my own good, but most anxious to follow out all I had been taught. To this end I learnt to speak fluently and to answer questions forthrightly, according to all that my observation had made clear. The state of sleep made me very aware of the causes that I unconsciously initiated. The effects also were made known, which when consciously understood gave me a choice of action and a possibility of using initiative.

The study of philosophy of any kind was not

encouraged, because nothing had to interfere with my writing up of conclusions gleaned from actual research. Proof found in this way was positive with power, for full determination had to be part of it all the time.

The way of life elucidated by personal observations had more than proved its worth. Its rewards, though not apparent in terms of worldly wealth, have been positive in many other valuable ways.

9. PEOPLE IN CAGES

My next experience was one that could have frightened me greatly if I had not had good friends to help me in my work, and in trusting them, had my lot made easier. My eldest son was then about twelve years old. He was studious, and in his own special way was also very helpful to me. On the afternoon of the day in question I was visited by two plain-clothes policemen, who, having been informed that I was a medium, wanted to find out just what I did. When they left the house after some talk, each held out his hand, and with this action a blessing on me was sealed, for both stated very firmly that they knew I was sincere, so had nothing to fear from them.

With these comforting words still in the forefront of my mind, later I retired to bed. The room was unusually dark, but nothing prepared me for how dark it was going to get. Music was coming from a neighbouring house, and it carried on into the astral consciousness. My eyes tried to penetrate the inky black, but I gave this up when I found I was walking in the open air.

I then noticed my son walking beside me. He was a little afraid of the dark, so when lighted windows came in sight we quickened our pace. However, we did not reach the windows, but were drawn by a very dark place that looked like a pit in the ground. I peered into it apprehensively, and then saw a flight of steps leading down. My son became even more nervous when he found I had to descend into the darkened pit. His words could have brought me out again, had not my inner self been in control.

"Are you going down there?" he said. "Aren't you scared?"

"Yes, I'm deadly afraid," I replied, "but I have to go down. Only by doing so can I find the way out, and that's what I have to teach."

I slowly made my way into the pit, which seemed to expand as I went further down. As I reached the bottom I saw people staring at me out of cage-like structures. They seemed surprised that I was free. Then I thought I had better go to the surface again and began floating upwards to the top of the hole. As I did so, some of the cages were broken down and the inmates managed to take my arm, clinging on to me as I began the upward ascent. This took much less time than the descent, and with even more people holding on I came out into the night. Two men on the surface made a grab at me but I managed to push them aside, and with an unusual strength of voice I shouted, "My God will not allow me to stay down there."

How glad I was to be out in the free air with all the people I had been able to rescue. The sky above us was like velvet, and happiness and lightness were natural to it.

Such is life, its many pitfalls cannot always be seen. Man does not know the pull of them, and often goes joyfully into a pit, not realising until caged that he has been trapped. Years were to pass before I would see the light and feel really part of it, still having a great deal to learn. Tuition came from many sources, I just had to be aware on all levels of consciousness to see what part of the inner self was affected. It was then that I found the brain a potential enemy to the Spirit, and that the freedom of the Spirit was – from man's own choice – unknown.

My many good friends included most of my family, who brought comfort to me while I was carrying the weight of tuition. My mother and sister encouraged me greatly, my brother also wanted to follow the way of the Spirit. But even so I didn't easily speak about the depth of my dreams, for today there are many who say, "Take no notice, it's only a dream."

10. A CANOPY OF FLOWERS

The years gone by held both beauty and happiness; they held also the ugliness of war and its aftermath. Still, this book is not a narrative of war, but a creative soliloquy upon events that took place during that period.

In teaching my pupils about the truth of life, I have encouraged them to learn how to journey uninhibited in sleep, and so to help themselves in everything they wish to accomplish. Frustration does not bless; it takes away one's powers of achievement. Training the mind to lay the right cause, the outcome shows more in the night, but is better for the body than anything achieved in the daytime.

In the process of development it can be found that the growing soul light seeks to enlarge itself, and is encouraged to do so during sleep, as and when the brain allows freedom. The *Poor in Spirit*, whose light is frail, are often the dominated of the earth. These are people held down and perhaps devoid of happiness and peace. In the Sermon on the Mount it is said that they shall see God. Penetration into the subconscious mind of the meaning of these words can bring the self into beautiful places in the spirit world.

There, the subconscious mind becomes steeped

in the radiant colours of flowers and the beauty of birds singing in the trees. Colour blends with colour, subtly changing and continuing to change, bringing added loveliness by the creation of multifarious patterns.

Many people maintain that they do not know what they do when asleep, and my reply is always, "The brain can be the self's enemy, barring the way to all that could heal the sorely-tried body."

The wisdom of the words, 'Be still and know that I am God', is not fully appreciated. Though receiving much respect on earth, the words if glossed over do not encourage the brain to participate in stillness and the help that can come from it. When trouble is its constant companion, it is very difficult to stop the brain in its circular thinking. At such times it is well worthwhile directing everything towards God, for the brain does possess an aptitude for stillness, the outcome of which is a natural asset to the earthly self.

When first visiting the *Chackra* states of consciousness, I was very sick – my body in pain and my brain hedged about with fears and worries. All this had to change in order for the work undertaken to be furthered. In promising to play my part, my whole prayer was, "Let me learn." I endeavoured to keep the brain still, but when it was not possible, I repeated many times the words, "I want to learn," until by reason of repetition all else was stilled.

[Editor's note: The Chackra states are the higher planes in the spirit world. Chackra is a different term to 'chakra', which refers to focal points used in some traditional meditation practices.]

I was well rewarded, for after a particularly difficult day I was glad to lay down to rest. At first my head seemed muzzy, yet sleep was far away. A vibration started in the nape of my neck, like the whirring of a propeller. The vibration seemed to grow in intensity and then accelerate. While still awake I was lifted from the bed and with a great rush of sound hurtled towards the wall. Fear gripped me lest I hit my head, but I was through the wall before there was much time to think about it.

It was a wonderful feeling, flying over the houses and trees. The landscape slid away beneath me as I flew on; it was exhilarating, and there was no room for fear. I felt my body being renewed, and rose to the process as all doubt left me. I had no idea where I was going but felt quite secure. The pace slowed down, and lightly as a feather floating to earth I came down in a sea of flowers.

I was standing by a bluebell taller than me. Laughing to myself I said to no one in particular, "I feel like Alice in Wonderland." Tree-like flowers grew all around and spread like a canopy over my head. And as my mind became more infused with the beauty of it, my dress altered in shape and in shade. With growing fascination I began walking, and great bells in various colours seemed to drop their fragrance upon me. The scent filled me like wine and made me so relaxed that I began to feel drowsy. Then I found myself once more in my comfortable bed, still able to smell the heady fragrance.

In the morning my memory of everything was very clear. I felt as if my whole body had been strengthened and there was no more pain. A distinct quietness of brain gave me peace, a far greater peace than I had known before.

From that time on, everything I saw in the earth plane took on a new significance. It was as if for the first time full appreciation of God was part of me, for now I could see God in every bird on the wing and every blossom hanging precariously from its wooded branch, heralding the fruit that would come after. I saw budding life, and in it I saw God.

With these things in mind I began a new phase of daytime activity in the unseen worlds. The night-time also became more purposeful, and there was a deeper significance in everything experienced.

Whether this was a prelude to what I was to witness later I could not say. The next day I was going with a party of ladies to a tea dance. The first part was uneventful. The time, however, gave me a treasure I shall ever see in my mind. The orchestra set up a very happy note, playing tunes from *Lilac Time* – the 1928 film. Suddenly I could see that the floor in the centre of the tables was filled with dancing fairies; the whole place appeared to be full of their presence. The colour around them was exactly the same as the bluebell I had been under during the night. My tea turned cold and the food remained untouched, so enthralled was I with the beauty in front of me. As suddenly as the fairies had come they left; I did not see their going. Other people wanted to know what I had seen, for no one else appeared to have witnessed the wonder of that fairy dance.

What beauty was shown to me on that wonderful afternoon, when my eyes could not leave the loveliness of those dainty creatures. People seated around me said how sad it was I had missed my tea. But sandwiches and cakes could never fill me as did the joy and grace of that fairy dance, which filled my inner being with food that has lasted for many years.

It was not long after, that another marvellous store of thought was given to me. It had been a pleasant day, and now the children were in bed. I felt it would be good for me to be in bed also, perhaps reading a book. The book did not hold me for very long, however, for my eyes soon closed, and in a moment my feet were taking me along the road in which we lived. When I arrived at the end where there is now a school and some shops, I found a scene entirely different from the one that I knew.

I had turned into a lovely lane, on the opposite side of which there was a grassy field. Wild flowers were everywhere, a bevy of beauty. I was very much tempted to pick the colourful array but something impelled me to begin the walk up a hill that lay before me. I enjoyed walking under the shady trees that almost met in the middle over the lane. The air was beautiful; just to breathe it in refreshed and stimulated me. I did not feel I wanted to rest, but wooden seats were fastened to the ground in between the tree trunks for those who needed to sit. What fascinated me was the ornamentation on the arms of each seat: lion heads, very well shaped, provided grip for elderly hands that might find difficulty in getting up. I had never seen anything like it before.

I was bemused by the beauty of this narrow lane. Slowly I came to the top. No one was to be seen until I walked over the brow of the hill, where there was another seat. A lady arose from sitting and came towards me holding out her hand. I knew her at once; her help during my school days was something I very much valued. Her name was Miss Kingston – I never knew her first name. I was very sensitive when at school, and the kindness of this charming teacher was just what I needed to break me from some of my fears.

After shaking hands with me she drew me towards a gentleman on the seat. He stood up as Miss Kingston introduced us. "This is Albert," she said, smiling at both of us as we shook hands. "Tell your mother about Albert, for she was so understanding."

My mother had been Miss Kingston's daily housekeeper, a treasure to the busy school mistress. I said I was very happy to see them and thanked my teacher for all she had done for me. But even before I had finished speaking I found myself back in bed, and heard the sound of my husband's key in the front door. I hugged to myself the lovely feeling of holding inside something that was going to be a joy to pass on, and I wrote down the details of the experience so that I might give my mother a full, word-for-word account.

In the morning I woke up full of happy anticipation. Hurriedly I went through the chores, and when I had finished I started off with the children in the pram to see my mother. It was a long walk, and on arriving at my old home my mother's suggestion that we have a cup of tea was much appreciated.

It was a happy time as I watched my mother taking in all I had to say. I took her up the tree-lined lane with the story of my experience of the night before, relating everything that I had felt. As I talked on she became more and more excited.

"I know the lane well," she said. "The seats were there when your father and I were young. We felt full of life after sitting on one of those seats for a while. God was there – we all felt it." There was almost a sadness in her voice. "Miss Kingston was a great friend. How wonderful that she would come back from the dead to assure me of her happiness." After a while she continued. "Albert was her fiancé. They were to have been married but he was killed. She lived a long time without him, but when she had to retire she felt she had nothing to live for and just gave up. How glad I am she is happy with her Albert; he was by all accounts a really good person."

The information concerning her friend stimulated my mother, and from then on she began to feel and see things for herself. She was overjoyed one day to tell me of something unusual that had happened to her. Apparently, she had been reading her Bible in the sitting room when she heard a light thud upon the floor. She looked up to see a lovely marigold lying on the carpet. There were no flowers in the room and the window was firmly closed. But the most amazing thing was the fact that this was in the middle of winter! And what is more, she had the marigold sitting in a small vase of water, proof that it was not merely a vision.

This happy experience was to be relived time and time again as my mother related it to the family and to anyone that came to visit her. After she had told me about it she said, "I always thought you were a rebel, but now I know why you were different to the other children."

11. THE COMING OF CHANG

My tuition was now coming rapidly, and I became more and more fascinated as I extended my knowledge and experience. At last I felt as though good progress was being made. Sleepstates were teaching me much and I was able to observe the results of causes made active in the night-time. Many things came as a surprise to me as I learned. However, the biggest surprise was yet to come and it was one for which I am ever grateful.

In order that I may tell you of it, I must go to the early part of February 1947. The weather had, I remember, been very cold, and I was sad because most of my friends were not in agreement with my desire to become a fully-fledged medium. There was a great deal of persecution, and this penetrated deep into my consciousness. No doubt it was because of this that I received the wonderful encouragement that was to come on a very fitting day – my birthday.

Considering that it was my birthday I felt pretty miserable. The only other person in the house that evening was my youngest child, fast asleep upstairs. I was sitting quietly in the dining room, feeling somewhat dejected and unable to think clearly because of all that was going on about me. In such a mood the emptiness of the house was all too apparent.

The previous Sunday I had visited the local church, and been very much dismayed at the messages being so lightly given. One lady, whose love for the church caused her to work many hours toward its upkeep, was not truly encouraged at all. This I thought most unfair, and became very unpopular by saying so. A further message given to a lady known to be conniving at her daughter's unhappiness, greatly encouraged her to go on; she was told she would win in the end.

I vowed never to be part of such a service again, and had been thinking in this way when a slight creak made me look up.

You can imagine my astonishment when I saw the dining room door opening, knowing full well that my daughter was still asleep. Quite breathtaking was the vision of a smiling Chinese gentleman, who came and stood just inside the room, shutting the door after him. His robe was green and yellow, but I could not see which was the predominant colour – my gaze being more upon his face as he advanced toward me. I do not know why I was not afraid and I still wonder about it today, but at that time I seemed to take so many things without emotion.

I was shaken from my own musings by the words my visitor spoke, and could hardly believe he was speaking to me. "Will you work with me?" he solemnly questioned, his face full of concern awaiting my answer.

His words were clear and said with such love and humility that I could not be afraid. This question was interesting enough, but I wanted to know more. "What will I have to do?" I queried.

"Just act naturally, but watch carefully every cause that you start. The effect from each cause will be our concern as well as yours."

Thinking I had nothing to lose by trying, I answered, "How do I know this is right? Can you prove yourself?"

"It will be difficult," he said firmly, "but I will help you to have materialisation six months from tonight."

Quick to grasp this, I asked him for the day and the date. Without preamble it was given, and smiling happily I accepted the proposition held out to me. Later, when I checked the date given to me in reply, I was astounded to find that it was exactly six months ahead.

He told me that his name was Li Chang Su, and this was subsequently shortened to the more convenient form of Chang. Little did I know of the many years over which he was to teach and sustain me when the going was tough.

I asked him what I should do firstly. He did not have to consider this for very long.

"You will ask your friend to sit in meditation with you each Tuesday evening. Be very regular. It is wise not to miss," he said. And this I agreed to do.

He made one thing plain before he departed. Very humbly, as if he did not wish to make me fully aware of the hardship that was to come, he said, "Your way will not be easy, for cause and effect cannot change until it is fulfilled. We must watch, and in time we will be able to help mankind through what you are able to do."

Just then what he said seemed to me to be unbelievable, and many times I have questioned it. However, faith has stood the test of time, and many are the experiences that have amply repaid me for the task taken on.

Thus was I warned that life would be hard, echoing Sing Foo's explanation of my vision of walking across a ploughed field, my feet getting heavier the further I went. I have found this to be all too true, but my feet are light when the body is left behind. Friends have blessed and given love, but there are many who would hold back truth, fearing to lose the substance that is theirs. In the Astral I have been challenged time and again, only to find that on earth, some paper or book written by me has floundered when putting it forward. Those in authority over the printed word fear the truth may injure them, rather than fill their pockets as hoped.

I remember when the News of the World gave me an interview, and a young journalist investigating Spiritualism became most amenable. I could see that through his pen some individuality might be expressed, although he was accompanied by an older man, set fast in his scepticism. The latter would not care if hurt followed the printed word, for his own soul was being crushed under the weight of discontent he carried as a chip on his shoulder.

Never was I more grateful for being able to see truth in the state of sleep than at that time. My inner self moved to where it could protect my interests as well as those of truth itself. On the night after the interview, I travelled through space and found myself in a room where the young journalist was busy at a desk. He was writing rapidly, as if he wanted to get it all down as quickly as possible, and be done with it. Moving round to see what he was writing, I found it was an untrue statement of his own findings.

I called his attention to what he was doing, and then for the first time his inner self became fully aware of me. Gone was the prejudice induced by the older man. Now he looked with seeing eyes, his expression softening as he screwed up the paper. Then turning to me he said, "I didn't know you had been hurt so much. I'll give you balm, so it may help to heal some of the pain."

Had the younger man been in harmony with the older, and both worked together, danger instead of success might have been the outcome for me. My heart was light as I went my way. How blessed I had been that the older man had no real love for his work, so proved no impediment to getting the report of my work altered.

Today there is an even greater hazard, for so many are afraid that truth will oust them from their positions of prestige. Only last night, when asleep, I was visited by a group representing the staff of a specialist journal. All were concerned with getting rid of me, because of the written word that I was trying to bring in. They said that I must be put out of action. Two of the men grabbed my arms, a third one held my head still, while a fourth pushed a hypodermic needle into my brain. Laughingly, they then decided that I was completely out of action.

But such is the power of instant healing that it was working almost before they had gone out of the room. Being outnumbered makes it harder to gain strength over others and so protect oneself, but the might of God can still work, and the truth approaching this world prove formidable to people such as these.

Cain lives on, his action copied by others. Unknowingly, desire to put other people out of the way activates the subconscious, and truth itself could come dangerously near to annihilation on the earth. Truth cannot die, and all who use it live of Spirit, for they are not afraid when tongues wag and goodwill is left to smoulder and die.

12. THE BIG SURPRISE

Having agreed to follow Chang's instructions, I arranged for my friend to meditate with me on Tuesday evenings. I was most surprised when at the first of these sittings there was a peculiar sensation at the nape of my neck. Then Chang started to speak through me by using my larynx. I had some idea that this was being done, but when the voice stopped I had no idea of what had been said.

This type of light trance is easily brought on by the spirit concerned using the brain of the medium. This happens far more often than the whole body of the medium being taken over. Using the brain is not dangerous for the medium, and the spirit can move away quickly should the necessity arise. Great danger has been with many mediums of the past when going into trance. With myself however, changes have taken place and these have proven many points for those of Spirit who wish to work with willing people of the earth.

The weeks went by and Chang became widely known as more and more people asked to hear him. Before very long we had established a group of seekers, all wanting to learn the particular way of life taught by such a teacher. Chang showed great love and respect for all those who came to listen, no matter who they were. Since that time however, his truthfulness has caused some to resent his words. Having something to hide, these people have dropped away, not wishing to carry on with their tuition.

As week followed week, varying visions and dreams were showing almost every aspect of our progress. This proved beyond any doubt that something very much beyond the philosophies of the past was to be expounded, and yet it was to incorporate the Bible and its deeper knowledge as understood by the Prophets, as well as by Jesus himself. The simple logic of cause and effect (as explained by Chang) became a very full foundation for everyday life, and many came to seek peace because life had floundered for them. Carrying out suggested measures, each one proved to their own satisfaction the value of living in such a way that peace flows outward from the self, bringing in return a greater fund of understanding and happiness.

So interested did I become in registering cause and effect in other planes of consciousness as well as the earth, that the months passed swiftly by. Excitement was in the air as the night of the promised materialisation drew near. The first hint that the promise would be fulfilled actually came the week before, when peace and quietness were with the small seated group. A kitten, black with white paws, came into the middle of the group. Chasing its tail and rolling onto its back it gave every sign of being alive. Everyone laughed at its antics and wanted to stroke it. Having heard previously that it is not wise to touch a materialised object until given the appropriate word I allowed no one to touch the small creature. It was then that a glint of colour made me look down to see a ruby ring near my feet. The temptation to pick this up was great, but even as the thought came into my head it left without being put into action. The time was not right for the handling of such objects.

The kitten vanished as our minds began to focus upon the ruby ring. Soon after I had the thought of picking up the ring, it too disappeared. One or two sitters who had seen this phenomenon wanted to put the light on to hunt for the stray kitten they expected to find, but they searched without success.

We were all left with a feeling of joy and excitement, looking forward to the following week with great anticipation. Having seen such marvellous things we began to wonder what sort of delight was to be seen on the actual night that Chang had given.

The following six days seemed more like six weeks to all those who were to be present on the big night. I was constantly having telephone calls from people wanting to know if Chang had given any further information regarding the materialisation.

I told them that Chang had stated there would definitely be a full materialisation, but he had not given any details. We all had to content ourselves with this until at last we came together on the appointed night.

Naturally we were all very excited and rather reluctant to become quiet. The atmosphere had caused the desire to talk, but eventually a good deal of hushing one another in good humour brought silence on a very happy note. Chang had taught us that tolerance is the keynote of all philosophies. Without it there could be no philosophical groundwork and no basis for the pliability which is so necessary for support from the Spirit.

Quite suddenly I was no longer present, for my inner body had moved away from my matter body. Afterwards I was told what happened next, that into the centre of the group came a beautiful young woman dressed all in white, carrying a lily in her hand. The scent of it was so powerful that it could have only recently been cut from its place of growth. Long, fair hair fell down over her shoulders and her smiling face revealed perfect teeth. There were gasps of astonishment as she stood and looked at everyone, and each made her welcome. She blessed them and then faded from view. As quickly as I had gone I returned. For some moments the sitters sat stunned into silence, until suddenly everyone started to talk at once. They told me excitedly of the visitation they had all seen. I was somewhat disappointed I had not seen her, but being more than glad that Chang's words were true I began to ask questions concerning the lady.

Mrs Cowen, someone who had been with me from the beginning, gave me the information for which I was hoping regarding the young woman's white robe. "Oh, but the gown turned blue!" she said excitedly. "It matched the blue of her eyes."

This confirmed for me the identity of our spirit visitor and I was able to explain that I knew her to be Lily, the spirit helper of Mr Charles Botham. He had been a splendid medium some years before, and he came to my group not long before he died. His sick body received much comfort from our compassionate people. Lily had been with him in his wonderful demonstrations at the Wigmore Hall in London. This place was frequented by many, who had witnessed his out-of-body experiences during which he would describe the houses that he entered and the furniture he could see – all with his inner body. He could even tell the people what was being said at that time in their houses!

Everyone present was delighted by the events of our evening together and looked forward to further visits by the same lady. That was not the arranged plan, however, and a good deal of explaining had to be done to keep the happy atmosphere when it was known that the teaching did not include week by week materialisation. Despite this, all were convinced that Chang had proven his words, and each one was very well aware that his teaching through myself over the weeks before had proven him genuine, and no one now thought of him without love.

Since that time the watching of causes and their subsequent effects has given a knowledge of vital facts. These facts have only been proven by the sincere and truly honest persons who wished to travel the full way of progress. Such words could appear to be biased, but one's inner self can be a part of oneself only – no matter what religion, theory or philosophical study one chooses to follow. The way is yet singular and determined only by the manner in which one lives the life that each and every day brings.

Week by week we sat for the education that could be received. Also it was required by Chang that I should continue giving two hours daily to meditation. This meant for me a truly wonderful time. Not only could I leave my matter body in the chair and move about the world quite freely, but my inner body also knew which people had to be met and was able to understand them, whatever nationality they were. I began to carefully catalogue my observations, as this was now the point at which writing had to be commenced.

Every condition I met in life brought an out-of-the-body experience. These were sometimes frightening, and yet at other times they were exquisitely sweet, giving a great deal of evidence that the nature of an individual is the only guide to their own experience in the earth life. Many times my teaching has been questioned, but proof can only be found and seen as the philosophy brings its own comfort.

The way in which writing came to me was not considered to be grammatically good. I found, however, that by other people altering the sentences without checking with myself, the context of the experiences was often changed. The decision was made to learn as much as possible about the setting out of words in order to avoid alteration. Since that time selected individuals have worked with me. The effect of this has been a simplifying of all the work involved, and many have found satisfying experiences after undergoing tuition.

During meditation, in accordance with loving spirit friends working within the framework of the *Project of the Golden Ball*, I was escorted to dimensions of thought where astral conditions do not prevail. Hell is not some far off distant place. It is the result of a build-up of earthy conditions as fear puts pressure upon the brain. One's own outlet from fear is the full joy of love, unhindered by sexual desire, which is a chain in itself. The one-mindedness of true love is the aim of all who would be happy. To reach this state of mind, with or without a companion, is heaven, and the brain being stilled allows only the inner being to be the guiding factor.

[Editor's note: The Project of the Golden Ball was commenced many years ago in the spirit world, with the aim of teaching people how to be at peace. The golden ball represents our earth world surrounded by the purified aura that true peacefulness can create.]

13. THE ANGEL

My life was not easy. I found difficulty sometimes when I least expected it. One night after an enjoyable evening reading auragraphs (pictorial representations of the aura) for people, I went to bed late and was somewhat exhausted. Sleep seemed to be waiting for me, but so were two men once sleep had allowed me to move out of the matter body. I appeared to be walking along a road, the stones beneath my feet difficult to walk upon. Without warning the two men gripped my arms. I then felt a ferocious kick, which sent me through the air to land on all fours, scraping the skin off my hands and knees and looking forlornly around for someone to help me.

The sequel to this dream came unexpectedly on Sunday morning. My daughter had suggested a visit to her sister. It was a lovely summer morning and hurriedly we dressed and went to catch the bus. There was no warning of what was to happen later. The visit was a happy one, my eldest daughter very pleased to see us. Suddenly I noticed the time and said, "We must hurry – I have a church service to do at three o'clock. I do not want to be late." It was quite a walk to the bus, and we started to run when seeing it coming along. Just at that moment my arms were gripped tightly and the kick I had felt in my dream I felt again. After almost flying through the air I came down and slithered along the stony path before coming to a stop. My legs and hands were skinned and bleeding. The conductor of the bus came and helped me and put me on the seat just inside the door. No one would have believed me if I had spoken of the truth, and so I kept quiet about it and thanked him for his help.

On arriving home I disinfected the cuts and bruises and bandaged my knees after cleaning the dirt from the lacerations. My daughter could not understand how or why it had happened, and I had to tell her that I myself was at a loss until I could meditate and be informed of the facts by a teacher. In any case we hadn't time to ponder upon the subject then, for I yet had lunch to prepare before getting to the church meeting. After cleaning myself up I said, "Nothing will stop me this afternoon." I found healing already commencing, pain being kept to a minimum.

It took an hour to get to the church. By the time the service commenced I was feeling no discomfort. In my address I talked of the soul and of how, when it is active, it can do far more good than the calling upon discarnate people who are not always working for one's good. Without the soul, mediumship cannot reach the same peak of wisdom that will help the poor in spirit, and also the mourner; neither is it possible to be meek before God yet strong before men. I did my best to teach the congregation of the great help which lay within each one of them; the rest was in their hands. I must confess that I wondered just how much notice they would take, for they most certainly showed no sign of sympathy about my accident, or appreciation of the fact that I had still made the effort to honour my booking and not let them down. As is so often the case, most seemed to be present just for taking, not for giving.

When I arrived home the discomfort of my wounds had returned somewhat. Night was far spent when I went to my bed with the day's difficulties seeming to be pressing down upon me. I started to weep, saying, "I can't go on." I did not know I had fallen asleep and that it was my subconscious mind causing the tears.

In what was now a dream I found myself walking along a road in the darkness of night, fearful of what I might meet. Walking blindly on, my eyes stung by the tears I could not stem, I noticed the road appearing to get lighter with every step I took. Suddenly the light flooded about my feet and spread in every direction around me. I had to shield my eyes, and then, growing used to the brightness, I opened them to see the most striking person approaching me. He was tall and handsome, with flaxen hair, a vision of beauty.

He turned and walked beside me; tearfully I looked at him. He walked gracefully, the long folds of his robe moving with him. Light in texture, it seemed to be moulded to his form, so that it was no impediment when walking. His eyes were a vivid blue, full of light, almost as if reassurance came from their depths. He put his arm lightly round my shoulders; my feet felt rooted to the ground as he turned me slowly towards him. I felt so ashamed. But as he looked at me my whole body lost its tension, and the burden of thought harassing it just fell away. Speaking quietly, yet with a firm conviction, he said, "Do you really think you can't go on?"

Stammering through my tears, I answered with a long and wavering, "No. There's nothing, just nothing left."

He began to smile, and I felt as if it was now a warm wing around my shoulders. His next words were so simple, yet through all the years of turmoil they have been my constant companion. "Do it for me. Can you do that, just for me?"

Nodding my head, for I could not speak, I felt the gentle and warming pressure on my arm increase and with it still there, I woke feeling heartened. Later I was told that this was the Angel Gabriel. I have not seen so blessed a figure since, but I have felt the comfort of the encircling arm a number of times.

Little did I know then that conditions were to continue for two years before changes could be made in my daily living, but the important thing was that I now did not feel quite so vulnerable.

Further encouragement came that night, for later in my sleep I had a visitor whom I call the Man in Grey. I gave him this name because he was always impeccably dressed in a light-grey suit, very well cut, and sporting in his lapel a carnation that looked perfect.

Straight away he started to explain the events of the day, saying, "Certain astrally minded observers were angry, because they had every intention of taking away the free will of the ladies who sit in the development circle at the church. Their lives could change for the better because of what you told them. The intruders knew this and wanted to put you out of action."

Such were his words that I was very happy I had kept that appointment.

Although the two years that followed were difficult materially, I have to say that blessing was present in the sense that whenever anything was badly needed it always arrived. Many repeated the words "God will provide", but the power of creation is used through the mind of man, and when love and appreciation are not present the power of the light is not in any way used to make provision. Much courage was given me at that time, and it increased when I continued to find myself blessed with experiences where, as I have mentioned previously, pound notes would invariably come out of nowhere when I was desperate for food for the children.

When one blesses another by word of mouth and is very sincere, all that is part of the mental self is very much increased. Blessing does not mean an increase in the things of the earth, unless the mind of someone is open to receive instruction to bless another. When this happens, blessing is given to the giver. That which is given is often increased. Should one lose something precious to oneself and carry hurt within the self for years afterwards, blessing is removed and perhaps more could be lost. If one gives generously by blessing that which is lost, and if one hopes that, rather than having been stolen, it has been found by one who has prayed for help, then great is the blessing and great is the colour in the aura – as peace and not resentment floods the mind. Should one in life give away only those things that are useless and broken, one will find on passing from this earth life that the home inherited is furnished with the broken pieces that one has previously given. One indeed receives as one gives.

14. THE MINISTRY OF ANGELS

Angels of light do not always have wings! Yet distance is no problem for them; they can pass through the sound barrier and to move at the speed of light offers no great challenge, for they move as fast as thought. Certain people when sound asleep are angels of mercy. Other people might not know their identity, but by their love and service they can be well known. Dedicated nurses, doctors, and many others who serve with love – these are all too often unsung heroes of the earth. Love is given by them, but they might not always receive love and blessing in return. In such circumstances they are the Poor in Spirit, as others dominate and use them for their own ends. Such angels as these, who work in the earth giving generously of themselves, are from the highest planes of life. Yet they must come through the womb of a woman, the matter brain having to learn through all the stresses of life before their ministry can commence.

To understand the reality of life is to understand the use of wisdom in all that is done. Wisdom comes from the inward part of the self, the brain unable to use full intuition. Resources outside the self feed the brain, but the inward self has no other food than the light that the colours in the aura may be able to produce. Not always do the resources feeding the brain bring to it the truth, and such are the difficulties many face that the truth of life is waylaid, leaving their ministry with no possibility of having a firm foundation.

Of one such case I was fully aware but was unable to save life. A wonderful person was the young woman concerned. She worked hard and got together a comfortable home. She rarely talked about the help that she had given to other people, but many have a home of their own because of what she was able to do for them. She kept in a book the names of those to whom she gave a sufficiency of money to put a deposit upon a house of their choice. The people repaid her, with no interest, when they found it possible.

Unfortunately, the young lady's husband was not of the same generous disposition and resented what she was doing. Though she suffered from severe headaches, she continued to work, finding pleasure in what her income allowed her to do. However, the persistence of the headaches led her to me. I tried to help her but found I could not remove the cause. I was able to see bad feeling coming from the husband because of his coveting his wife's earnings. Neither she nor he knew that when both were asleep he could use methods of persuasion that brought on the pain.

One night in my sleep I saw him beating her about the head. She was pleading for mercy, but he was merciless. I was not able to catch her as she fell to the floor, still trying to protect herself. Suddenly she lay still, and he looked at her then left. I could sleep no longer that night, and when morning showed its light I telephoned to find out how she was. She was dead. The death certificate showed the cause of death to be a cerebral haemorrhage. No doctor, however, would know that it was not truly a natural death.

Before the funeral the husband was collecting the monies stated in her book. He threatened court proceedings if the people did not pay up. But causes bring their effects, even though man tries to close his eyes to them. When the husband thought he was all settled, he fell sick and was in a great deal of pain. An operation could not save him and he was called to face the effects of his actions, an Angel of Mercy conducting his encounter with the natural comeback of his mind's machinations.

The man's return to earth as a discarnate brought no comfort. He was not encouraged to go back to his home, for those to whom he had willed it sold the property, and when he went to go into it he was locked out and could not enter. There was nothing he could gain upon which to survive from those who were loving and happy who occupied the house, for his own state of mind meant that he was closed to giving and therefore closed to receiving.

What is not altogether understood is that when the soul of a man dies because of his own actions he himself will then commence to die, for the flesh relies upon the inward self for full life. Without the soul, which is the part of man that is of the light, man would not long survive.

In my investigations I have seen good, bad and indifferent behaviour. The time of sleeping shows the truth of man's being. He can hide everything in the earth, but when he is asleep he is limited by what he is and how he behaves where other people are concerned.

A day of unusual disturbance gave hazard to me from which I found great difficulty in finding the power of light to offset the effects of it. My husband, having come through pneumonia, was found to have tuberculosis. This was a great blow to myself and our young daughter, (our fourth child), who was especially close to him. It meant me having to nurse him at home. There was one evening when I had to fetch some medicine for him. The blackout was causing the dark night to be even darker. I knew nothing as to what was going to happen on the way back home, which was some distance from the bus stop. A man detached himself from the people waiting for the bus. He followed me. When I hurried he went faster; as I slowed down he did the same. I had not brought my torch with me so was unable to light my way. My mind sped ahead – what should I do? A large park with gates open wide was only a few yards ahead of me, and I feared he would push me in. Arriving at the gates, and without thinking, I ran out into the road and screamed as loudly as I could. Doors opened, lights flashed; the blackout was forgotten but the man was gone. I was saved.

Of myself I felt sure my inner self had inspired me, urging me to act quickly and to move away from danger. Unfortunately, some time later two young women coming home from late shift work were attacked and almost killed. Before that sad event my experience had been thought to be a hallucination.

On going to bed on the night of my near miss with the would-be attacker, fears became too great for me and I found comfort in weeping. It seemed as if I was being released from the pressure of mind that had been built up; this was so that it would not enter my subconscious self and become a menace to me in my inward self.

The following morning brought to me extra comfort that showed the ministry of angels extending to animals as well as humans. I awoke early, around half past five, with sunlight streaming in through the bedroom window. There, stood at the foot of my bed in the bright light of the new day, was a lady who appeared to be in her forties. She was dressed in a beautiful magenta-mauve crinoline dress and her hair was in the pompadour style, with jewels hanging in the front and two ostrich plumes arranged at the back. To my upliftment and joy, she was holding Sandy, my small, well-loved dog who had passed away about two years before. The little thing immediately sprang from her arms and into mine. He nuzzled and licked me, just as he had done when he was in the earth plane.

"You have not found accommodation for him yet, you know," said the lovely lady. "You must make proper provision immediately."

I was somewhat taken aback, pointing out that when Sandy had passed away I had asked if he could be allowed to reincarnate as a farm dog, to enjoy the freedom and open-spaced life I had not been able to provide. The lady informed me that this was all very well, but I had not made any arrangement for the affection between Sandy and me to be eased, which was essential for him if he were to start a fresh life on this earth. Apparently there was still a strong mental link between us, and my regular thoughts of him added to that link. In fact, it had taken almost two years for my memory and thoughts of him to ease sufficiently for me to be approached concerning him.

I recognised the sense in what the lady had said and thanked her for bringing Sandy to see me. I promised to let go of him mentally, hoping that he would have the chance to reincarnate as I had originally wished. Now that I knew how his future happiness rested upon my releasing him, I was able to bid him farewell with a new joy.

It was just over nine months later when I saw Sandy again. This time it was in the state of sleep. I found myself standing at an upstairs window of a school building, looking down upon the playground. Children were running about, and there amongst them ran little Sandy, happy as could be. I was told by a gentleman that the dog could not see me through the glass, but I was not sad at this, for I knew that his mind was at last free of the link with me that had previously impeded his progress. The man said I would not see Sandy again because he was soon to begin his new incarnation. Although this was the final farewell, I was happy to think that my small friend would soon know the beauty of being a dog of some import in a place where life would be fine for him. And how wonderful it was to see the help that loving people can be to all of life, for both Sandy and I had been blessed.

Much of my work was in the state of sleep as well as during daylight hours. For when people came to put their problems to me it was often at night that I was able to get at the truth of the matter, and so settle seemingly hopeless conditions. Obsessions and possessions were many, not only with airmen who found themselves awkward in the company of other people, but also with those who had been near bomb blasts and were somewhat shattered and unable to think clearly. An obsession is where a spirit interferes with the brain of an individual, while a possession is where a spirit possesses the body as well as taking over the brain. Using the light from my inward self, I was able to see the unpleasant misty green which is visible when an interfering spirit is made to move out of their victim. Indeed, without the light it would be difficult to remove them completely.

❖ ❖ ❖

Lying in bed one night, I was pondering over the various problems that had arisen that day. Learning how to be a teacher was indeed a rough and stony way. My mind went to the loving angel whose encouragement had spurred me on, but there was soon to come a greater encouragement, one that I would never have dreamed of receiving.

The figure came silently, like a shadow, until at the foot of the bed I saw the Master. I was astonished to see this image of Jesus before me, colour and light playing around him like fairies in their gossamer robes. His face was serious and yet kind, and in his arms a tiny lamb nestled. He looked at me with eyes of love and said, "Feed thou my lambs." And then a second time, "Feed thou my lambs."

My eyes went to a picture hanging on the wall, one I treasured. The figure in my room was not unlike the artist's impression of Jesus in that picture. For love was with him, showing himself in a form that enabled me at once to understand the blessed goodness he represented. His words gave added life to me and I accepted the challenge. It would be hard, I knew that, but just how hard it has been is known only by my teachers and myself.

I was astounded by the light and the feeling of peace as this wonderful man looked at me. He was one who used the Christ Mind, the high quality of thought that all sincere, loving and true seekers use when their inward self is able to lead the way. I was dumb before him, but the tender look in his eyes refreshed me and no longer did I ponder upon problems. I wanted to shout from the housetops that I was to serve, but first I had to learn how to love and how to spread it about me, remembering that lambs can easily stray. As the figure left me as quietly as he came, I felt humbled before such a visitor, and I prayed I would have the courage to do what was required of me.

15. THE APE

In my capacity as a medium I had to travel to a church some distance away, necessitating staying for a couple of nights. There were a number of other people there with whom I felt in harmony; each was looking for a way of life wherein the Spirit played a major part. It was delightful to be in like-minded company, but my wonder was surpassed when I saw a gentleman talking to a small group, his back turned to me.

For a moment I did not know what to think or do, having recognised the back view of the man in my courtroom dream. My first impulse was to thank him for his timely support.

It was almost as if I was back in the sleepstate, the authoritative calm of the speaker swinging me back in time as the group eagerly conversed with him. His words were accepted and not challenged, and I felt humbly grateful that the inner self of such a positive man had accepted the responsibility of helping me with the work that had made life so hard. His name, I learned, was Len Brooks.

Sleeping under the same roof the first night had brought little to endorse the interest shown in the previous sleepstate where, as it were, we had first met, and when I was formally introduced to Mr Brooks, he showed no recognition of me at all. I realised that to tell him about my experience would consciously commit him, so it was not mentioned, and he took little notice of me as the day proceeded.

That night proved very different. When sleep came, I found myself in an express train travelling at high speed. It was a fine day in the dream, and though the earth body was asleep, the inner body was so natural that one could easily think it was one's earth body in an unusual setting.

The windows of the train were open, and – typical in dreams – the most illogical things were happening. Along the side of the track there were stalls supporting a variety of goods. My fellow passenger, Mr Brooks, told me to take whatever I wanted, adding, "You can have the lot if you like."

My response to this invitation was, "I mustn't take it all, or others will go short."

When I awoke from this powerful experience I was greatly humbled, for I realised that every personal help was going to be given. What was required to pursue the work would come, and from that time forward it would take on a protection so far lacking. Under protection it would widen and so help many others in the same way as I had found help. Such were my thoughts, and from my heart I gave grateful thanks.

None of this prepared me for the next episode as, with every anticipation, I once again sought sleep. I was sleeping on a put-u-up in a comfortable semi-basement room. In one corner was a large cupboard formerly used for storing coal. I had felt no apprehension at being alone in that part of the house, so was all the more shocked when the cupboard door opened and out shuffled the largest ape I had ever seen.

It was led by a man holding tightly to the rope looped round its neck. Slowly they approached my bed. I was hypnotised; I could not move. With dried mouth I tried to scream, but no sound came. In slow motion, like something from outer space, the huge animal moved as the man jerked the rope.

The man was smiling, so I relaxed a little, but wary of a trick I watched him closely. In his hands he was holding a vacuum cleaner. I had long wanted one in my home, so would not have been surprised to learn that at long last I was going to receive one. Cautiously I sat up in bed, my arms outstretched to take the gift offered.

At that moment, the menacing creature sprang forward, and with bared claws ripped open my back from neck to base of spine. The laceration was not clearly visible because of the quantity of blood spurting from it.

Still smiling, the man backed towards the cupboard and disappeared. The ape just faded into nothingness as I found my voice and screamed. Nobody heard, for this was my inner body. Coming out of the experience I spent some time in meditation and prayer, whereupon the shock began to leave me and I knew the lacerations to the inner body were healed. I know now that if healing had not taken place I would have got up in the morning in great pain. No doctor could have diagnosed the condition, and relief might have taken a long time.

Such a startling experience could have remained shrouded in mystery, had not the truth of these things been made known to me. For since that incident, many people have laughed in my face or been sympathetic whilst ruthlessly tearing me to pieces behind my back. In being withheld, the vacuum cleaner – a symbol of easy work – has meant unnecessary hardship. My need of the appliance was used to draw me to a sitting position, so that injury could be inflicted. In such situations instant healing is essential.

My determined endeavour to clarify certain fixed ideas were often thwarted and hindered, because the facades of people did not portray the striving of their subconscious minds. The efforts made to take for the body sufficient to satisfy its desires are not realised when the brain is coveting what others have. Such was later found by our research group that painstakingly worked to secure the full truth of positive cause and effect.

Few people know that lower animal life predominates in planes of consciousness below the earth. Man's use of the animal kingdom is not confined to the daylight hours; in fact it can be far more prevalent while the subconscious is using the inner body. I have seen many animals used to intimidate people, observation of the astral self having been my main concern. Covetousness is the link with intimidation, hurt to the body being so greatly feared that by these methods the covetous can secure what they desire, the expert handling of ferocious beasts having supreme advantage.

At first I was inclined to think I had seen a vision, but actual marks on my back, despite the healing, proved otherwise. Protection gained by means of cutting desires within myself, resulted in better health and a more relaxed way of thinking, which subsequently aided many experiences that might otherwise have brought pain.

On speaking of my experience at the breakfast table a ripple of humour passed through the company, and after voicing incredulity the subject was changed and the matter quickly forgotten.

After the weekend services were finished and I was preparing to leave, I found that beside me, Mr Brooks was the only member of the group travelling to London. He had planned to take a later train, but decided in favour of an earlier one, so that conversation with me upon themes of the Spirit could be enjoyed.

I found him utterly sincere in all that he believed. He was earnestly seeking an understanding that really worked in life, having been much disillusioned in philosophies having no practical application. His interest had been stirred by my addresses at the services, and he surprised me by relating an incident that happened the last time he slept at the place we had just left.

Apparently he had been wakened at 3 a.m. by a large ape approaching his bed. He had jumped up and put on the light to find himself alone. He did not mention the incident or the fact that he had walked about for the rest of the night. His reason for not speaking of his frightening experience was because of his reluctance to cause worry, because so many people enjoyed visits and slept in that room. His words distressed me, for I wondered how many others, seeking the full course of the Spirit, would be similarly intimidated and perhaps put off forever.

It seemed that Mr Brooks had promised a thousand pounds to go toward the work, which was anticipated by those present in the group. They would not be aware of their natural powers when the influence of the subconscious was put into action out of the body; from continuous subconscious thought, the possibilities are beyond belief. Intimidation is becoming rife on earth now that the brain is put to more and more intellectual expansion. I had been intimidated so that there would be no menace to those already hoping for the help that could be theirs. Since then, it has been found that many have come under intimidation when wishing to be generous, for always there are those who covet.

Few people understand that where vows are

sincerely taken, the inner self accepts the responsibility of them in the Astral. Promises given when out of the body carry even more responsibility in the eyes of the Spirit than those made on earth, and can bring serious disturbance when broken, or great blessing when honoured – for one can be raised from the Astral to a higher part of the spirit world once fulfilling a promise.

That return journey was a wordy feast. Len eagerly grasped everything about the way I had been taught. He recognised the philosophy as something akin to himself. When we parted, he promised to attend classes and learn from the beginning the way of life as taught by us at our centre-cum-sanctuary. He kept his word, not only coming himself but bringing friends whose hunger was as great as his own.

16. THE RAT

Material benefit is often thought to be a blessing from God, whereas it is merely the outcome of cause and effect. The cause, set going by oneself or by spirits, brings an effect to suit the body but is not always beneficial for one's spirit self; in fact it can be a block to it. Subconscious power and the use of spirits in sleep were proved to me at this time, when many conditions were altering. I was asked to leave the house I rented as it was now up for sale. This was a real blow to me, not least because this was where our sanctuary had been set up, at that time named 'The Sanctuary of the Rising Spirit'. It had happened to others, but I had hoped it would never happen to me.

Conditions of life being turned over in another's mind can provide a base on which spirits may prophesy. Thus it was prophesied to me that I would leave my home and work in a factory in the North! How glad I was that there are two types of spirits; those who further the path of enlightenment on earth, and those who go to great lengths to deter it. Taking this prophecy to the Masters in Spirit, I was not surprised to hear that if I went away I would be brought back with ignominy, for the work in London was not yet complete. The prophecy had been the opening gambit of someone wanting to shift me prematurely, but the message had had a ring of truth.

So I stayed put, and from then on circumstances began to move more rapidly. I find this is possible if blessed spirits can trust and be sure that one will await the next move. After being persuaded in sleep that to move would be a good thing, one might accept this with relief and so miss the greater chance that being patient could bring. Proof of the strength of higher spirits once more came at night, and from what was received I knew it was wise to follow out exactly the suggestions made.

A sleepstate set me pondering; the dream was not specific, but its content was sufficiently logical for me to unravel the symbolism and find the core of truth. I found myself walking along a thoroughfare where a market was being set up. One man drew my attention to a chicken he had, pointing out its good food value. He offered it to me, holding it up by its neck and saying emphatically, "Two thousand, five hundred pounds, and not a penny more." As I took the fowl he repeated with further emphasis the price. I noticed that I had to prepare the fowl for the oven; it was not already done, as in the shops today. Every feather had been plucked, but otherwise it was not ready for cooking. To me this meant there were things to be done before receiving any benefit. I pondered on this, then decided to wait and see.

After being given the chicken I walked along the

road to a bus stop, and seeing a bus in the distance, waited for it. With a laugh the driver ignored my raised hand. Some time passed before another bus came and I was able to board it. I did not remember getting off the bus or at what point I left the chicken behind, but finding myself back in bed, the sum of money stated was engraved on my mind.

The morning post brought the answer. As a sitting tenant I was offered the house for £3,000. The meaning of the dream slipped into place, and I wrote at once offering £2,500 as recommended by the Spirit. The subsequent correspondence ended in deadlock, and the passing bus was made plain. I could do nothing but wait. Having been told a definite sum, I stuck to that, though where I was to get the amount troubled me somewhat, for if it were to be agreed upon, what would I do?

My mind reverted to the promise of help in my dream of the courtroom. Was this the area wherein it would manifest? I know now that I was wasting mind energy, in that keeping my brain active took its toll of everything progressive, frittering power and detracting from what was badly needed by those who wanted to help me.

The switchback of life continued. I learned in a breathtaking way, thrilling to speed in the night, and yet held down by the earth and the fear invoked in me as each day brought the causes from which the night would show the effects. Everything about the way of the Spirit held me with interest. I could not have broken away had I tried, though often finding myself the centre of antagonism. The up and down was caused far more by my reaction to circumstances than to the circumstances themselves, and through this I learned not to build the bridges of life before meeting up with them.

By this time the sanctuary was open for both healing and teaching, although numbers in attendance had been dwindling. I had put it down to bad weather, and had no suspicion that adverse circumstances were putting pressure upon people. At the desire of some of my members, a medium was invited to take a group. No warning note sounded as to the outcome of pleasing these friends, and happily I made the arrangements. The night was cold but inside was warm, and a friendly atmosphere seemed to make a glow about everyone. After the medium had received some refreshment, we all settled down to enjoy the evening; still no hint was given of what was about to take place.

The medium was popular with everyone, and laughter rang around the room as in jocular fashion he spoke to each person present. I began to breathe a sigh of relief, but deep within felt that something momentous would happen.

Suddenly the medium stopped talking; everyone looked expectantly at him. With a laugh he looked at me and said, "This has got me beat, but I have to say it." My stomach turned over, wondering what was coming next.

The medium looked searchingly at a little woman, and then quietly said, "And so, you have been driving out the rats?" He laughed, and so did we all. No one thought of the seriousness of the situation or of the effect that so few words would have upon the whole of my specialised career.

An equally quiet, "Yes," from the woman, accepted the words as being understood.

The medium continued, "And the greatest rat of all must go?" A nod came from the little woman, but her face changed completely as the medium pointed at her and said, questioningly, "You?" Laughter still carried on, but there was a perceptible change in the warmth of the atmosphere and soon the group came to a finish, no one seeming to be very interested in the refreshments that had been prepared.

Unfortunately, as I closed the door on the last person, I overheard a remark from the little woman – who was waiting outside. "There, what did I tell you," was all I heard; I did not want to hear more.

Closing the door quickly I returned to the medium's somewhat awkward apologies, but he – being sincere – soon forgot his embarrassment and said with a smile, "Well, perhaps it had to be said; I trust all will be well." I assured him that it would, and enjoying some of the dainties I had made for the guests he showed his appreciation of them by his entertaining conversation.

17. A VITRIOLIC LETTER

A sequel came two days later, when, for the first time, I arranged to go with a friend to visit her sick daughter in hospital, instead of taking my two-hour meditation. Failing eyesight prevented my friend from going alone. On opening the front door to go out, it was as if a great force struck me in the stomach. There was nothing visible to be seen, but clutching my abdomen I bent almost double and slowly had to go back inside. The moment I was sitting down the pain left me, and with a sigh of relief I said to the room at large, "So I did not have to go out. It would have been easier if you had told me!"

A laugh met my words and a quick rejoinder flashed back to me, "You would have taken no notice if I had."

Since that time I have realised that what one wishes to do is often stopped, simply because we make no firm arrangement with the Spirit prior to the decision. My helpers were regular in their attendance and they expected me to be the same, a ruling with which I now firmly agree. I did wonder what made it so important for me to meditate on that particular day, but the answer came quickly enough.

I had not been long in the chair when two lovely

young women came in, dressed in the style of the 1920s. One wore a bright yellow dress with a long fringe hanging down, which swung gracefully when she walked. A yellow hat fitted snugly upon her head. An exact replica of the yellow dress and hat graced the form of her friend, whose lovely smile is with me yet, except that a glorious shade of apple green was the colour that matched her auburn hair. I had to smile inwardly at the hats they wore, for this took me back over the time when I myself had worn a similar style. Both laughed delightedly at what was being done to me. I laughed also when one said to the other, "Do you think she has gone off?" I could have told them I had not, but they didn't ask me and I silently continued to enjoy their chatter.

I was glad I was not asleep, for at that moment a little man came in wearing only a loincloth and a turban; the same one who helped me escape from the courtroom. He started to busy himself, prodding and manipulating my stomach. I wondered whether he was giving me healing, but soon understood I was mistaken in thinking healing was the main need. He pulled something from me and held it up. Concentrating my gaze I saw a letter, written on blue paper and burnt round the edges as if someone had confined it to the flames and then retrieved it. I realised it had been written by someone with disturbed emotions, and knew it would contain some very unpleasant words. It made me feel uneasy, but the little man laid a hand firmly upon my shoulder and with a smile assured me that I had nothing to worry about.

He put the letter on one side and again probed my abdomen, this time bringing out an egg almost as large as an ostrich egg. I looked at it amazed, trying to figure out how it had happened, when he said, "Good. She is ready. When this hatches out there will be a lot to do." My brain was getting active. I had thought I was already a busy person, my phone constantly ringing as one and another had dreams not decipherable to them, but obviously I was not busy enough. Still, I was glad to think I should not be alone in what was yet to come.

Delivering the egg was later explained as the beginning of a new phase of the work for me. My meditation had to continue so that further experiences might be undergone. In the future this could help other people to secure the way of the Spirit, as they sought to find the answer to their earnest seeking. My experience of the afternoon was so firmly entrenched in my mind that I could not help but tell my family of it on their arrival home. They did not share my enthusiasm when stating there would be a lot more work to do.

Toward evening, people began to come in. I had a large group on a Friday at that time, mostly those who were interested in research into the unknown. At that time my teaching was tentative, for I was very much afraid of giving tuition contrary to truth. It was nevertheless an exciting time, as the inner body of one would go to another and speak until most of the people in the room were making conversation with their inner bodies. I did not at that time know the full value of the aura or understand the power that came from it when the colours were bright and harmonious, but I did realise what wonderful harmony could be achieved when like-minded seekers were together.

Just as we were about to start the group work, another seeker arrived. As I opened the door to him I noticed an envelope on the mat. Having a premonition that this was the scorched letter seen in the vision that afternoon, I took it into the kitchen. Len, the young man who had just arrived, followed me. The letter was written on blue paper without a signature, but the handwriting I recognised as belonging to the lady singled out by the medium at our last meeting. It was an example of what is today called hate mail.

Many accusations against me were written down, and within the words it was possible to see the emotional struggle that had led up to the putting of pen to paper. She evidently wanted Len to love her, and considered me to be standing in the way. Emotional fire had consumed her, making it plain as to why I had clairvoyantly seen the pages scorched and burned at the edges.

As I read the venomous content my heart went

out to the misguided woman who had written it, since her suffering was obviously intense. "Poor woman," I murmured. "If she'd only come and talked with me. She must be very unhappy to write such a letter."

Len took the letter and quietly read it through. When he had finished reading he looked quizzically at me and said, "Aren't you angry?"

"Why should I be angry?" I replied. "I feel sorry for her. She can't hurt me, but it is unfortunate that she is hurting herself."

Len looked at me and said, "At last. You are the one!"

I was puzzled and wanted to know what he meant, but we had to go in to join the others. I felt sure that after the group session he would tell me everything.

There was no occasion to hide the letter from the rest of the group, so I began by relating my own experience of the afternoon, then gave them a summary of what the letter said. Learning from it was essential, and it proved to be of interest to everyone.

One lady who had been at the previous meeting said, "So this is why we were told you were closed and seeing no one." She had not wanted to worry me, and so had said nothing until then, but it seems that buses had been met and information passed on concerning my eventual closure. Indeed the medium was right, for those in disagreement with the more progressive teaching I was introducing had been persuaded to stop coming to the sanctuary meetings, and now the woman described by him as 'the greatest rat of all' had herself withdrawn.

In all of this I could see but one point – the beginning of a further cycle of life; the new undertaking to be class work only, with no public services in the sanctuary until a sound theoretical understanding could be reached, giving a basis upon which everyone could be taught and harmony prevail. The letter could have depressed me, but I saw in it release. I felt a new state of being would come in, the work now depending solely upon myself with no support from outside mediums. I was elated, but still realised that a good deal of change and hard work was yet ahead of me.

Len and I left the rest of the group in the social room with their sandwiches and tea, and once more returned to the kitchen where he commenced his narrative.

"I came to the earth for a purpose," he said. "Some time ago I was a Roman soldier. Since I could think for myself I have lived with the thought that I have to pay reparation, specifically to a young woman who was a Greek at the same time as I was that soldier. You see, the girl was burnt at the stake and I could have helped her but did not.

"I have been observing you and a number of other workers for Spirit, praying for guidance to be certain that my desire to serve Spirit is fulfilled. Sadly I have often been disappointed, because some who speak well and seem sincere fall down when it comes to the vital test of honesty and truthfulness.

"I can't explain how exactly, but I believe you are the girl I could have helped before. The way you reacted with compassion to that horrid letter showed me that you are genuine in your teachings, and I feel that you are the one I'm seeking."

I was somewhat surprised by this, but my own experiences had taught me to value past incarnations.

"Do you own this house?" he continued.

"No," I replied, "I pay rent, but I have been told to negotiate to buy. Six months ago I was told to pay £2,500 and not a penny more. The owner wanted £3,000. I have paid no rent since this commenced."

"That's it," he said very firmly. "I have to get a mortgage for you. How glad I am my search has finished."

My knowledge of this man was such that I trusted and respected him. He was very practical and down-to-earth – definitely not the sort to spin a yarn or lead anyone up the garden path. My inner feeling also told me that truth was being spoken and that he was entirely sincere. I thanked him for his good intentions, but he simply expressed his gratitude for the opportunity to fulfil his quest.

The eventual outcome of these circumstances will not be recorded here, for they digress widely from our narrative. Suffice it to say that with Len's timely help I was able to buy the house for £2,500 – the price given to me in the dream of buying a chicken.

18. AN EXORCISM

An interesting sequel to Len's revelations concerning a past incarnation of mine came some time later when returning home after taking a Sunday morning service, I had to answer the telephone. A man's voice begged me to come immediately.

"She's crying in the cupboards and on the stairs," he said. "It's awful. What can I do? I can't see her!"

I said that I should like to help but couldn't do much that day because of having another service to take that evening, which meant quite a journey.

The voice then pleaded, "We will do all we can to help, but please come. We will give you tea and then take you to the station."

At that entreaty I said I would be there at 3 p.m. It would be an hour's bus ride from my home. With a few words of thanks he rang off, and I had just time to see to my family before making ready for the journey and the service to follow.

The journey included taking three buses, but I arrived at the house on time. A gentleman opened the door as I was going to knock a second time. He looked at me queerly and I wondered whether I had made a mistake in coming. Quickly he pulled himself together and invited me in. His wife was very pleasant and we sat around the fire chatting.

Apparently, I was the thirtieth medium that had been asked to come. None of the others wanted to take on an exorcism.

The gentleman went out of the room, saying he would not be a minute. When he returned he was carrying a framed picture. "No doubt you wonder why I reacted somewhat strangely on seeing you," he said. I nodded and he went on, "I have painted this portrait of a woman in Greek costume and was told she was burnt at the stake."

He then showed me his painting of the woman. The resemblance to me was striking, and she was dressed as I had seen myself in a dream. I knew at once that the Greek incarnation spoken of by Len was a reality, and that I had indeed suffered death by burning! I was amazed by this confirmation.

"Can I buy it?" I asked.

"I'm afraid not," he replied. "I have an exhibition very soon, and this picture is going on show. I treasure this portrait, and will be treasuring it far more now because I have met you."

I understood that he should want to keep such a remarkable piece of evidence, and I felt greatly privileged to have seen the likeness.

After that introduction we started meditating upon the lady whose crying was upsetting everyone. She soon came to me, and though no one else could hear or see her I could relate what was being said. I asked her who she was and why she was crying. No one was expecting the discourse that was to last some minutes and horrify us.

Two men had taken a room in her house, and they made themselves comfortable and appeared to be helpful and kind. However, after going one week to collect her pension for her, they kept the book and other monies coming in for the letting of the rooms. They said they were keeping it for her, and persuaded her to sign everything – including the house – over to them. She questioned them one day about a paper she needed and could not find, and said she would have to go to her solicitor, whereupon they hustled her to the top of the house and locked her in a small attic room.

They fed her meagrely and allowed her no contact with people outside. After she died she returned to the house and so frightened the men that they sold the place, and everything of value that was in it. This didn't stop her being unhappy, but when the artist and his family took over, they, being spiritualists, knew she was there and were very kind. She felt comfortable with them and was able to do as she pleased in her old home.

"I was very happy," she said, "until I heard them talking about moving."

"Are you moving?" I asked of the artist.

"We have thought of putting the house up for sale," he replied, "but so far we haven't done much about it."

At these words the little woman started again the wailing of despair. I had to quieten her. It would be necessary to get her consent to go, and I sent up a prayer for the White Brotherhood to come for her. The Brotherhood comprises loving people who help those who are clinging to the earth to move on to a new and more progressive life. I told the woman of the little cottage she would have by the sea, and how warm and comfortable she would be meeting all her old friends.

Just then, two brothers from the Brotherhood arrived. "Her son is coming," one of them said. "Just let her know."

I realised that though I could see the two brothers, she was on a lower level and could not see them. I told her that her son was coming for her, and the two of them would be together for a while. When her son came in there were cries of joy. The two from the Brotherhood gently held the woman's arms and, accompanied by the son, lifted her up and commenced to float upwards. At first she screamed and her legs kicked the air, but after her initial shock she allowed herself to be taken, departing up through the ceiling. Love had come to the poor woman at last; it was the key that unlocked the prison of her own house.

I sent out a thought of thanks to the White Brotherhood and saw a brilliant green, the green of love, flooding the room. This episode is just one small part of all they do.

The artist and his family were very happy, and for the first time since thinking of moving house they had an unbroken night's sleep. The experience taught me a very great deal which since then has proven of benefit to other people. Love is indeed the key; without its use I would not have been able to learn or to do the things I have done in this earth world and in the worlds unseen.

19. TEN YEARS YOUNGER

Pursuing the course of investigation, I felt at one time that my life was almost lost. No one could advise me and many tried to persuade me to give up my efforts. Allowing myself to become despondent I was wide open to spirits who wished to deter the work. I had been feeling very unwell and one night, as the August Bank Holiday of 1959 approached, I found myself having to go to bed early due to my condition. Almost immediately I fell into a deep sleep. Feeling no relief and appearing to be still awake I was yet totally aware of all that was happening in the bedroom.

Suddenly my body was held fast. It would not move. Beginning to struggle to free myself, I saw two unpleasant-looking men laughing at me. A woman stood near them and she had a book within which a number of names were written down. After looking at the book she pointed at my inert body and, shaking her finger in emphasis, said, "Take her to the sacred crocodile of the Nile. She can be our next sacrifice!"

Coming back to myself, I called on Chang to advise. On his face was an expression of concern, and trying to assure me he spoke softly. "Do not go into hospital," he said. "That is all I can say. Keep calm and great will be your blessing."

Having already made an appointment for an examination I thought that all would be well as long as I did not go in for treatment. However, the terrible discomfort that I was feeling was such that in my bewilderment I was only too relieved to give way to the insistence of the concerned doctors. Therefore, although it was Bank Holiday Monday, I had to enter the hospital for an operation. From that time on a dream-like state seemed to possess me and I no longer knew what was going on around me.

In the worlds unseen, however, it was quite a different story. I was very much aware of being bound up like a mummified figure and of being hypnotised while many voices chanted. I was beginning to feel drowsy and thought, 'This cannot go on.'

Then mercifully I knew no more. Some time later I awoke to feel terrible discomfort, while a nurse put ice to my lips. I had been barely conscious for five days.

For what seemed like months (but was in fact only weeks) I lay there, the doctors not allowing me to sit up in bed. The two unpleasant spirits returned again and again to mock me. However, I gradually pulled round and was told that something had gone wrong, and that after recuperating I would need another operation. Having been told this, that night felt like the longest I have ever had, but towards the dawn I was overjoyed to see three purple-robed spirits sitting at a longish table floating in the air above my head.

Each one looked up from writing in the large books in front of them. They smiled, and I felt comforted immediately. My face must have been a picture of questioning, for at last one said, "You will be quite all right, leaving hospital in a week; do not return." I felt strength coming into me as I thanked them for coming. I somehow knew I could trust their words and would feel better and not die as was expected. They smiled once again, nodded and disappeared.

During the day Chang appeared to me. Laying his hand upon my shoulder, he thanked me for all that I had allowed the spirit ones to witness. He said that great value would be added to the spirit world because of that which had been observed, and very soon I would be blessed for all the troubles I had gone through.

The next day I spoke to the surgeon about going home. He shook his head but said, "I will examine you and give you the results in five days." He went into detail about the type of operation I had undergone and what had gone wrong.

"But I did not come into hospital for that operation in the first place. You asked no one for permission to change it," I said.

"It is done now," said the nurse in attendance.

The surgeon then remarked, "Now you need rest, and in six months you must come back for another major operation. It will be necessary."

I found my voice. "You may be sure I shall never come back to this hospital and you will never operate on me again. I will see to that."

He laughed. "You will have to." He thought he had me in his grasp, but remembering my visitors I was quite sure that operation would never take place.

It was when I was in this poor state of health that once again the unpleasant spirit men came to mock me. They did not know to what extent I had been strengthened by the words of Chang and his fellow investigators. Perhaps I too would not have known of this strengthening had the two bad spirit men not appeared. For the first time since entering the hospital I told my depressive visitors to go and pester someone else. They quickly turned and left, leaving me to wonder why I had not been forthright before.

Later in the day a friend laughingly described a visit which had been paid to him, and it explained quite a lot. Mr Ernie Brice was a very talented artist and a very staunch supporter and student of our teaching. At five o'clock in the morning, in his sleeping state, he heard a phone ring and found himself to be in the sanctuary. In answer to his question as to who was there, a gruff voice said, "Your boss sent us to pester you. This is Mr Lousy speaking!"

In explanation I had to tell him that I had

said, "Why don't you lousy people go and pester someone else?"

Our laughter rang throughout the ward; to me it was a dawning light. The night passed and with it melted all the terrors through which I had been.

Proof of unintelligent spirits can be found as unprecedented sickness strikes the unwary, who by reason of being emotional break down their own protection which is so necessary in this astral plane of earth.

It is needless for me to say that the blessed love of the Spirit was made manifest and I left the hospital on the sixth day, promising to rest and do nothing around the house. The following day was a red-letter day for me as my younger son was arriving from Australia, the RAF having granted him compassionate leave.

Many visitors arrived during the day. By the evening I was tired and in need of rest. The group had continued to meet at the sanctuary and an outing had been arranged. They were to go to a séance to witness the work of a well-known physical medium, but had wanted to see me first. Finally, they reluctantly went on their way, leaving me alone in the house.

The experiences I had that evening easily compensated for any that my group may have had, for the medium appeared to have little power to uplift them, whereas I myself found great and positive joy. Chang was my first visitor. He was obviously well informed, as straight away he spoke comfortingly. I had to carry on meditating from two till four every afternoon to gain material for what I had to write – a very rewarding time.

"Now you will be able to open the school and teach," were his opening words.

This had been promised me when I was being encouraged to meditate. Many experiences out of the body had taught me, and new written lessons had now to come from that which had been learned. Chang saw my brain working and carried on in his own quiet way, "Your house will be the school. Train mediums to teach philosophy. It will be proven to be a support to all in mental or physical need."

The idea to me was wonderful but I spread my hands in dismay. "How can I open a school without a whole body with which to work?" I asked.

Chang smiled and said, "You will recover and find yourself able to manage financially, to repay you for all you have given. Do not let anyone take advantage. Everything is possible. Have faith and believe." Smiling to himself as though he had some hidden detail up his wide and elaborate sleeve, he went out and I settled down to rest.

A friend had said she would come and sit with me. However, she did not come, and I was left to ponder over the wonderful thing it would be if I was really able to open a school for the help of people who were seeking. I was passing my time idly in this manner, when suddenly the door opened and a further spirit visitor arrived. With his white loincloth and turban that stood out in the now darkening room I recognised him immediately. The light that was giving way to the night was still sufficient for me to see a greatly oversized pill in one of his hands and a glass of water in the other.

My eyes goggled at the size of the pill. "What will that do?" I gasped, finding it very difficult to get out the words.

"It will take ten years off your age," he said quite simply.

Holding out my hand I took the pill and put it into my mouth, apprehensive of its size. I was surprised at its sweet taste, and how it melted and became easy to swallow. Offering the water, my visitor indicated that it should all be taken. He then said quietly, "Now rest." I cannot explain the feelings I had at that moment. It was as though a great contentment filled my being and I hardly noticed this dear one leave. His name I later discovered to be Krishna, though not the one associated with the Hare Krishna movement. I have been informed that this wonderful friend of mine was closely connected with the more famous of the two when he lived on the earth, in India. His main interest is in the development of the philosophical literature, and he continues to be a source of great strength and encouragement.

On arriving home my family came to my room, and seeing that I was asleep they went away again. I did not wake until the next day. The light seemed to be bright and golden. I hurriedly put on my work clothes and thought to catch up with the many things that were left undone.

In the bathroom the laundry basket was overflowing, and taking it downstairs to the kitchen I happily did the washing and pegged out two lines of it. The pill was working fine, I felt young and lively. When I felt it was time for the family to get up I looked to see what was in the fridge and found bacon and eggs. The rich aroma of bacon soon brought them down.

"What do you think you are doing?" my husband asked. "You are supposed to stay in bed for a month." I laughed and told him what had happened. He was overjoyed to hear it.

"I'm here on compassionate leave because you were going to die. Now look at you, you look a million dollars," came from my son.

"Some pill, that," laughed my daughter.

Nothing more was heard from the hospital or from my own doctor, so nothing was ever checked as to the result of the operation. In my heart I blessed the wonderful men in purple robes – members of the *Purple Brethren* as I found out later – and above all Krishna, who had taken ten years off my age and given me a new start in life.

[Editor's note: The Purple Brethren are a

dedicated group of people in the spirit world who look after the pool of animal life force, in addition to advising sincere seekers of light who are subject to persecution.]

20. THE HEALING SANCTUARY

It was not only vitality that I felt – other changes were apparent. The lines of pain had gone from my face and my hair was changing! Up until then it had become dull grey and lifeless. It took a few days for my hair to change colour, but after washing it I found it had become much lighter and full of life. Excitement was growing as I telephoned first one and then another to announce that classes would continue under my instruction. Many to whom I had spoken could not wait for their usual meeting night and decided to visit me that day.

Sunday being a good day for getting about, the sanctuary was very soon full of people. Sometimes they were all talking at once, sometimes they were all quiet, thinking about the miracle that had happened. Towards the evening we were engrossed in deep discussion about the ways and means of passing on to other people the wonderful encouragement that we ourselves were receiving.

Our cup was indeed overflowing, and we felt that we could do no less than open our doors to all who needed love and healing as well as tuition. Having agreed on this everyone went away happy, but I found out afterwards that I had made a grave mistake. I say this because I had been asked to commence classes but in effect I was opening a centre for healing instead. At that time this did not appear to be in any way against the Spirit. Very soon, however, I realised my error as more and more letters started to arrive.

Requests for healing came at all hours. I found myself getting into debt, for although some people put a donation in the plate, others took out what they could when no one was watching. I made no charge for private sittings, relying solely upon the generosity and goodwill of the sitters for donations. Here too there was discouragement when I found that many had placed only a small coin in the plate for an hour-long consultation. Disappointed and much disillusioned after working in this way for two years, I gave up and went out to work to repair the damage, financial and otherwise, that had been done to myself and my family. They somewhat relied upon me, because my husband was unable to work due to ill health as I have already stated.

My work for the Spirit had never really been accepted by my husband; he could not fully understand why it was so important to me. As time went on the distance between us mentally grew larger and larger. It was decided that it would be better all round if we parted and went our separate ways, following our own desires and interests.

Just after he left Hendon I found two spirit friends awaiting me in my room. One of these was Krishna and the other was Zambala, a tribal chief who was greatly interested in healing. I sat on my bed and waited for them to speak. I was fascinated to see the difference between the two, Zambala being big in stature, fleshy and very vital in his attitude to life, Krishna on the other hand being quiet and inoffensive but very wiry and spirited.

Zambala's huge body was shaking with laughter. I had no idea as to what he was finding so funny. Suddenly he picked me up in his arms and laughing loudly threw me up to the ceiling. He tossed me up in the air as though I were a child, and my cries of distress did not seem to reach his ears because of his hearty laughter. At last he seemed to tire of the sport and he put me down.

When all was quiet Krishna spoke: "Forty years have I waited and now this!"

His words shook me badly for they were not for Zambala but for myself. His eyes did not speak reproach in any way, but from his manner I felt somewhat uncomfortable. Zambala looked crestfallen. I tried to think of something to say but I had no idea what Krishna meant. Finally the penny dropped. I realised that Zambala and his healing had grown so big that it had made everything extremely difficult for Chang and for the teaching I had been asked to take on.

"I cannot drop everything just like that," I said, my confusion showing in my voice as I tried to see how a complete changeover of everything could be arranged. Once again spirit helpers brought circumstances under control, for an early morning job was offered to me. Taking this job enabled me to clear the way and advertise classes for two evenings a week.

Prior to this time the classes had not been specific. However, commencing with lessons upon development and differentiating between full development and partial understanding, I found happiness and stimulation. Yet I found it difficult to realise that the friends who wanted to heal and whom I had been teaching in the class should be much different. It had not occurred to me how much additional work and responsibility would have to be taken on for development classes, and how much life itself would alter as truth was sought and found.

21. LEN BROOKS AT THE SANCTUARY

Time passed and everything regarding the mortgage was now settled. The house that Len had helped me to buy proved to be a blessing, for it served as a centre of love and tuition. Many happy hours were spent there with those who were genuine seekers of the Spirit. We held meetings and classes, and after these we would go into another room for tea and biscuits for happy and friendly conversation. I was content with the progress being made, and it seemed at last as though things were truly under way.

But for Len, other past and present complications now began to show themselves. Being a kindly man, he had promised help to a number of people and was doing all he could for them. This he continued to do to the best of his ability, sometimes going short of cash himself because of the greater needs of others.

Len learned well and blessed the school with his service. In return he was protected and made contented, but his love of people was so profound that when many of them tried to wean him away from the Spirit, and pressure was strong upon him, he did not fight for life.

The first indication of his break from the earth was given to him in the state of sleep; he was with his family on a bus, then suddenly realised he was quite alone. The family had left him to continue the journey on his own. From that time on, we watched carefully lest he became overtired. But despite our care, the mental persuasion upon him was to prove too heavy to bear.

Len was someone whose heart would go out to every sick child, and who would weep for every animal he found hurt or maimed. He had no resistance against those who sought to take advantage of him, and it fell to me to protect him as much out of the body as in it. A lady who said she had loved him for a long time began to be burdensome, for by the use of spirits she caused havoc in his life. Her emanations were strong, but in any case she was not free to marry.

The situation so worried him that he left himself wide open to hurt in the state of sleep. I know that if his distress had been understood by his friends it would have ceased. But few people realise the power of unintelligent spirits, who use one individual's emanations to inflict harm on another. The state of sleep became a battlefield for him, and I was asked to take a hand in the background of his life. To help with this, he became a resident member of the sanctuary.

It was wonderful to be able to talk to him and to others living at the sanctuary. Few of them understood Len's true love of the Spirit. His mother was gracious and helped him with her love, but his good name left him open to gossip that passed from one unenlightened person to another. My role of protector and friend had to cover a wide area, and it became the groundwork upon which much of our literature has been written.

Len was an excellent healer, but in misunderstanding protection he suffered greatly from his own resources of sympathy. It was difficult to prove this to him, because I was being watched over myself lest I encroached upon anything belonging to his essential experience.

The state of sleep was well known to me, but my students were only on the brink of realising the power of the inner body to alter conditions on behalf of the subconscious mind. Good thought is constructive; it is a builder of good faith and blessed conditions. Covetous thought is destructive; it strikes time and time again at the sincere. As a result, I found that not only Len, but I myself was under pressure from those who clung to the thought of receiving help from him. I had to tackle each one in turn, and without the light of God I would surely have been crushed, for the pressure increased when Len fell ill.

Sitting in a study group one day, Len went into a trance-like sleep. He was not controlled by a spirit, but had subconsciously initiated circumstances with which he had to contend. On returning to his body he was much upset, having travelled to a place strange to him, and been taken prisoner. After a while he had been led outside, stood in front of a wall, and shot. His body fell from him and he walked away, while loved ones came forward to meet him. He longed to look back at his body, but was told not to, as the killers were brutal and it would distress him to see what they had done.

A buzz of talk followed his account of the experience, and the general opinion was that he should have been more protected. The group had no knowledge of his complicated background, involving one person after another having to be broken away from him.

The experience had its inevitable result, for early the next day he arrived back from work with a pain in his chest at the exact spot where, in the experience, the shot had entered. I knew that speed was of the essence, so immediately took him into a room and helped him on to the healing bed. We had already agreed that prayer during the day should include help for him, and we were assured that it would be given. The pain cleared and one hour later he felt he could get up.

Suddenly he was seized with a feeling of acute nausea and had to rush upstairs, where he vomited violently. Tired after all that had happened, he went to bed. I thought it wise to get the doctor, who said that by vomiting he had cleared the blockage – and that had saved his life. The healing had helped

Len to survive, but as a precaution he was admitted to hospital.

When Len came out of hospital our students continued to work hard together. Len himself was a very practical man. He taught himself to type, and papers began to be printed regularly. Everything was settling into a fruitful routine, when we were very rudely shaken by an experience giving us some inkling of the covetous minds working against us.

Len went away for a few days, and my daughter and I were on our own. It is as well to note at this juncture that discarnate beings watch everything that is done, and take advantage when one is apparently unprotected. People passed over still love or hate as they did on the earth; there are some discarnate individuals who can be very helpful, but it is not always known what they actually do to gain the help their loved ones want.

I had never met Len's father, who had passed away suddenly, not having shared his son's interest. In my sleep I heard the crash of a breaking window and went into my daughter's room to arouse her. Such things can be done in the spirit environment, the activity of the inner body relying upon the astuteness of the subconscious mind.

Having woken her (though her matter body was still lying asleep) and made her aware of unusual noises downstairs, we arranged that she should stand behind her door with a heavy weapon, while I stood in the doorway of my own room. The waiting built up tension, and when at last a man came up the stairs, I recognised him from a photograph as Len's father. He was followed by a number of men brandishing heavy sticks and shouting that they would put me out of the way. Without Godly light to protect me I knew that I could have been found dead in the morning, and no one would have known the real reason.

Before the men had a chance to strike me I put up my hand. The front ones stopped as if some hidden shield stood between, whilst those at the back clumsily bumped into each other.

At this my assailants seemed confused. Some were inclined to still push forward, but no blow fell on me. It was then that Mr Brooks senior pointed out that he had not understood the situation and was sorry to have caused this disturbance.

Unfortunately the pressure did not finish on this note, for something else happened that proved the sanctuary was coveted by someone who had been much loved by Len's father.

My daughter and I were late to bed one night, having been some distance to serve a church. It was not long before I fell into a deep sleep, but my inner body was awake to the extent that I did not feel I was asleep at all. I left the bed and floated towards the door, making no sound as I went through it. To my surprise there was a young woman showing a man over the house and telling him what alterations she wanted done to it. I was extremely taken aback, having received no intimation of a pending move from the Spirit.

The woman went outside and furniture was carried in, then set down deliberately, as if much thought had gone into the arrangements. On this occasion I was not visible and preferred it that way, mentally noting that everything must now be done to secure my ownership of the house so that I could not be put out.

When Len returned I told him all that had passed during the weekend. At first he was certain no one would go against his wish to help me fully secure the house, but to make quite sure he paid a visit to his mother. He found out that the property was indeed coveted by someone in their family. This one felt that because Len had put down the deposit on its purchase, as well as making several improvements, she had a right to make her home there.

Because the state of sleep revealed the covetous thought centred on the property, it enabled us to safeguard our security further. But from that time on Len's health deteriorated. He had bouts of nausea and some pain in the kidneys, which he did not hide from me but kept quiet from everyone else.

22. THREE PEARLS

The year moved on and Christmas came. A number of old people were given a whole day at the sanctuary, waited on by our students. Nobody anticipated what was coming, and Len was in his element carving the giant turkey and leg of pork. The feeling of happiness was palpable, and left its memory with us even after the blow had fallen.

The persuasion put upon Len to lose his life came from a number of people, but in the end only two made sure that his promise to look after them would be carried out.

The first symptom was only a pain in his head. Due to past experience we called the doctor, who prescribed something for the headache and asked to be called again if anything further developed. During my sleep that night I found myself at a bus stop. I was accompanying Len, because he wished to visit some friends. He had no intention of staying with them, for he was already making arrangements for the work he wished to do on behalf of the Spirit.

The bus came along with an elderly couple on the open platform at the back. It stopped, and they beckoned to Len, who stepped onto the bus to greet them. While he was thus occupied, the man called out to me, "Give me three of your pearls and I will let him come back to you."

My physical self no doubt would have gladly paid out the price demanded and considered it money well spent. But one's inner self knows far more than the outer ever can, and without thinking, a very direct, "No!" was given to the blackmailer, whereupon the bell was pressed and the bus started, leaving me alone at the stop. I then awoke and had to push from my mind the thought that despite all efforts for Len to follow the way he had chosen, he had been enmeshed nonetheless, because of promises made.

The next morning I told him the circumstances, and he identified the couple. They had at one time been very kind to him and were now passed over. His heart had gone out to them in gratitude, and because of this he had promised to look after them should they at any time be in need. Len did not know, however, that this could be carried on into a further life.

It is not always appreciated that promises can be misused, and under certain conditions are most valuable to anyone trying to take advantage. Past teaching has not shown all the truth, for it has seldom been pointed out that in the Astral there is the need to eat and sleep. Someone has to work and earn the money to supply these necessities, even after the earth life has finished.

Having made a promise, Len had been approached subconsciously to keep it, which entailed his passing over in order to render the service required. At the time, I was puzzled about the three pearls, but now know that when one gives up pearls of wisdom one automatically surrenders what has taken years to acquire. In other words, one would retrogress overnight, in terms of loving advancement.

In a few days Len's condition worsened and he was taken back into hospital. Three days later at 10 p.m. he died of kidney failure. He was only forty-five. We were all somewhat shocked by the rapid demise of this dear friend. I particularly felt the loss, for we were very close and he had always been such a help and encouragement to me in my work. I resigned myself to the fact that he would no longer be around in the earth plane, but I did not realise that this tragedy was to give rise to another unpleasant condition, one which was to be most disturbing.

No sooner was Len dead than certain people took advantage of his absence to start extremely unkind gossip concerning me. I tried to carry on regardless, trusting that things would eventually die down. However, the gravity of the situation was made clear to me one night in the state of sleep. Although I knew I was in my bed, my inner body was up and dressed.

I walked down the stairs and out of the front of the house, and there I met the travelling companion on whom I had come to rely. He had supported me when the adventure first began. His quiet voice gave me courage and never failed to instil faith, for with only a few words he could give me confidence in the most meagre of opportunities.

We stood on the path leading to the house. Suddenly he turned, and walking into the garden, beckoned me to follow. He made straight for the large bay window of the room in which we had refreshments after meetings. He looked in, and I looked too. I was shaken by the sight that met me, for the room was completely burnt out! Blackened walls and floor sent up tiny wisps of smoke, but otherwise there was nothing left. His next words staggered me, for there was no hint of anxiety in them at all. "Don't worry. We will use the insurance money." He smiled as he spoke; everything I had was gone up in smoke, and he almost seemed pleased!

Frantically I tried to remember if I had kept the premiums up to date. Seeing my train of thought, he said, "No, no, my dear. Your insurance is what you have built up by your own endeavours. All that you have learned can be put into practice. You have friends who will bless you, and their love will see you through. From the rest, learn."

His assurance was infectious, and I found myself thinking: 'Oh well, perhaps it had to be.'

I have since seen numerous rooms in a burned condition, but at that time was somewhat new to the experience, and my understanding not so strong to cope as since that time. I knew from this that the place was being ruined by the fire of people's emotions, and the fact that the room was gutted showed the possibility of all my work going up in flames. I was being shown that the gossip would not fade out as I had hoped; it would instead be enlarged as the individuals concerned listened and passed it on. Regretfully, I had to accept that the answer was to leave the centre, my home, and start afresh elsewhere, all that I had established there being destroyed by idle tongues and undiscerning minds.

23. LEN'S FUNERAL

I very soon had the opportunity of knowing that Len continued to live and was not far away, for when taking the service at the crematorium, I was delighted to see him sitting on his own coffin swinging his legs. He was wiping his forehead with a handkerchief in mock horror at the heat into which his discarded body was to go. His presence made me want to laugh, somewhat out-of-place at that solemn service, his friends and family having no real idea of his work for the spirit world. The chapel was full of Len's friends, who shook hands with me and thanked me for the service. "Delightful," one said.

Soon after that he returned and spoke to me, the old familiar voice saying, "Hello Glad." He also put my mind at rest, as I had done nothing about putting a plaque to his memory in the crematorium. He said that as he was in reality not there and would not want to be there, it didn't matter. I was just to keep on with the good work and not let anyone stop me.

Some while later, he arrived by my bed one night and spoke in the voice we all loved so well. He was in a light-hearted mood and said jauntily, "Come on!" holding out his hand so that I accepted the invitation. I had thought I was awake, but my inner body rose from the bed and away over the rooftops we sped. It was a thrilling journey, over the roads and fields and little cottages, until at long last we reached the sea. Coming gently to rest on the seafront we looked around. The sky was blue and the sun shone clear overhead. I looked up and saw a castle standing upon a hill, gleaming in the sunshine.

"This is where you will come to live," Len said. "You'll recognise it."

His words caused me some concern, having worked so long to build up the sanctuary in London. My dismayed thoughts dispelled the state of sleep, and I found myself thinking these things over in bed, with Len nowhere to be seen. I was sad about that, feeling that somehow I must have cut down the time we were enjoying, but I had been assured that I must learn from all experiences and then all would be well. One's own thoughts can break valuable connections. Sometimes, however, a quick exit from a dream has proved to be of great benefit, especially when one is in a tight corner. As I lay thinking, I felt I could not wrestle with the problem, but must leave it in the hands of blessed ones. Much was obviously being planned.

This dream gave me upliftment because it showed that I was not left completely alone, wandering aimlessly; there was a sense of direction, and patience would show the way. I did not recognise the scene that Len had shown me, but

I knew that I would find the place.

In the sanctuary I noticed that people were becoming distrustful, for they left themselves open to the lower type of spirit, and it was hard to come out unscathed from the resulting conditions. My motives were continually questioned, and so burdensome did life become that I began to be happy about the prophesied move, whereas previously I had been sorrowful to think of leaving behind those I loved.

Once I had made up my mind that a speedy move would ultimately be the best thing, I found myself thinking of ways and means, and was doing so when drifting into sleep. This came only lightly, for in a few minutes I seemed awake again; someone had come through the door. I was somewhat perturbed at the entrance of a young woman who had been much trusted in our work. She had become a medium and was beginning to be known, but had herself been greatly disappointed in her conscious life, events not entirely falling the way she had anticipated.

Her conscious mind may have been totally unaware of the plan her subconscious was weaving, but the inner self was very purposeful in its desire, and her words to me very deliberate. "We can carry on this place," she stated, "there is no need for you any more. We have learned, and we can do very well without you."

With these words she went her way. I knew from

this experience that such things being so positively said, endanger the body, destroying health and probably reason as well. In my case it was done in order that the sanctuary would pass into the hands of those I had willed it to. Too late I saw the mistake I had made in making such a will, but when one completely trusts, there is no hesitation in doing all one can to prepare for the future.

However, in a way the statement was a relief, for I realised I had been somewhat foolish in trying to smooth the path, and also in trying to stop the forcing issues that were taking place. Knowing that all things had come to their climax, I began to set things in motion for the move away from London that had to follow.

Throughout the following day I discussed the situation with my youngest daughter, who still lived with me. That night I slept peacefully and awoke early in the morning with a sense of well-being. Then I fell asleep again, and to my joy found myself floating, just round my room at first, as if waiting for someone. At last he came, a young man unknown to me. He was big and very strong, his face alight with life. His hair was light auburn, beautiful to see. I must have been asleep, but I could see him clearly.

He beckoned me to follow him and through the wall we went, following the telegraph wires strung across the countryside. He warned me not to get too close to the wires but somehow they appeared to draw me, and at one point I caught my clothing and a piece tore off as I pulled it free. It was only then that I realised the torn-off piece was a different colour to the nightdress I had on when leaving the house. I looked at myself and saw I was no longer wearing a nightdress but a very pretty orange dress instead. Keeping a wary eye on the wires, I managed to steer clear of them the rest of the way, and was relieved when at last we came down into the garden of a house.

Without knocking we went into the house and made straight for the stairs, as if the rest of the house held no importance for us whatsoever. Mounting the stairs quickly, we reached a square landing where three women were stood talking. They were most surprised to see us and seemed as if they would like to detain us. But to my astonishment my companion lifted himself off his feet, and with no effort at all went through a trapdoor in the ceiling. He was so much bigger in body than the aperture through which he disappeared, that I was bemused and made no attempt to follow him. For looking at my bulky size and the height of the opening above, it seemed impossible.

We were all looking upwards when the young man's head appeared as he looked down through the hole. "Come on, you can do it," were his words to me.

"I can't get through that," I said, somewhat

stupidly, as I had a feeling he wouldn't give up until I was there with him. Without more ado I tried to lift myself from the floor but to no avail.

"Forget yourself," he said. "Don't think you can't do it, for you can."

The words put new life into me and my next try was successful. I found myself clinging to the sides of the opening. It was not necessary to think further, for automatically the body knew its own way and went through the aperture easily. I came out in a large room where I seemed to be expected. I was encouraged to go forward and told that all would be well, not to worry. And these were the words still being said as I woke up.

It was only later, when looking back upon this episode, that I could see how much it prophesied the hazards that have dogged me throughout my research. Many times have I been caught up in the emotional wires of other people, some of whom have almost destroyed the work. Long has been the time and narrow the way. Fear has stayed my hand, but my way has gone forward, however narrow it became. And as I write, still the words ring out, "All will be well!" Like bells in my ears the words resound, and I fear no longer, for all has been proven and found to be true.

24. HASTINGS

It was a few days after I had the dream that my friend Maggie and I took a coach trip to Hastings on the south coast. I was taking a few days' holiday and serving a church at the same time. Alighting on the seafront, we set off on foot to have a look around. Imagine my excitement when I glanced up and saw, on top of a hill, the very castle Len had taken me to see. Maggie was equally excited. We had agreed that she would move in with me, because she loved the Spirit and was very strong in her support of me and my work. There was the castle, an unmistakable landmark, and both Maggie and I were like two children embarking upon an adventure. We started straight away to visit estate agents in the town, gathering information on properties that might prove suitable.

Although we can have wonderful guidance, we still have free will, and not always do we make the right decisions. Len had blessed me with his loving guidance and had shown me the general direction to follow, but the more specific details were entirely up to me. I picked the house that I thought would make the best centre for my work. I was eventually to find out I had taken on a place rather too big to be easily maintained, but my move to that house and the early days there proved to be enwrapped in joy and anticipation of new and progressive life. In my heart I blessed Len constantly for all that he had done for me, in both his life on earth and his life in the Spirit.

Having to leave my centre in London was at the time a great blow to me, but I was grateful for everything I had learned there. It enabled me to find greater value in my new home, my past experiences helping me to avoid repeating certain mistakes that could have interfered with progress. What is more, moving to a completely new environment gave me the opportunity to learn new things that I would not have understood had I stayed in London. It made me determined to forget the upset of the latter days, so that I could bless this fresh beginning with happy enthusiasm.

Mr Ernie Brice, my good friend for many years in London, promised to visit me regularly to help in any way he could with the various work involved. He was as good as his word when the time came, and I shall never forget his help in our time of need.

There was one more joyful experience in store for me on the last night before leaving London. We had been extremely busy and many hands had helped us. The furniture was already packed in the van, ready to depart at an early hour. Mattresses were laid on the floor, on which I had my doubts about being able to sleep, but once settled, almost immediately I found myself in the spirit world with the companion of many past sleepstates, who seemed in a hurry to get going.

"Would you like to see your friend, Len?" he asked. "You won't have so good an opportunity as tonight."

I was only too willing to accept his invitation, and we set off on our customary flight through the wall and into the night. Until then I had thought – in common with many others – that there is no manual work in the hereafter, but I'm afraid this is a pipe dream from which I was rudely awakened. I had no idea where Len was, but my companion seemed to know very well, and was making straight for the place. As we went on, brightness faded and everywhere looked overcast. It was not really dark and yet there was a gloomy atmosphere.

We arrived at a very large building reminiscent of a factory, and I was surprised to think we might find him there. All was noise and bustle, none of the peaceful serenity that we had enjoyed together on earth. When we had to go to an office to make enquiries, I knew that Len had not found rest but hard work. My companion asked where Mr Brooks could be found and we were told to wait, that someone would go and find him for us.

When at last he appeared, I noticed his sleeves were rolled up and his apron showed signs of the heavy work he was doing. We apologised for bringing him out, but he said: "Don't worry about that. I'm glad of a short break now and then. Is there any trouble? Do you want any money?" he went on, but as he put his hand in his pocket I was already declining his kind offer.

"I have to work, but I like it," was his next comment. "Although everything is just as costly here as on earth, and there never seems enough to go round."

I could hardly believe my ears. "But surely," I protested, "there's no work necessary here. So many have said there isn't. Do you actually get paid for doing work here?"

He laughed at my naive questioning. "How else do you think I can fulfil my promise to look after my friends?"

My heart was sad when I left him, but my companion cheered me up by saying, "When he no longer wants to work like this and can really see beyond it, he will find a great blessing for being so kind."

Some years later I heard again from Len, telling me he was now in a much brighter plane of life with others who had loved the tuition I had been able to give. He asked if I would bring my work in the earth to a close, and go over to where they all were. He added, a little sadly, "We need teaching here just as much as in the earth, where teaching is not really appreciated." I had to say "No" because of wanting to stay in the earth until the feeding of the lambs I had been asked to do was really accomplished.

❖ ❖ ❖

The house that Maggie and I found in Hastings was large, and I truly thought I would be able to run a centre there. However, I soon discovered that my education was by no means complete, and my practical understanding was still insufficient to support the type of centre I had in mind.

Since that time, I have had to go from place to place to understand the full length and breadth of Spirit, and all that can be done when in sleep one's motives and inner senses rule every action. The subconscious mind is the ruling factor, its limitations causing the earth life to be left open to harassment and difficulty. Causes commenced when asleep may seem to be obscure, unless one is aware of the symbolic nature of dreams. Over the years, I have learned a great deal from watching what is started in the state of sleep, and then seeing the results in daily life. From such knowledge I have found I can discern more closely my own thoughts and actions. Thus I have become better equipped to spot and avoid many of the pitfalls that line the path of life.

As I have said, I chose the house at Hastings according to what I had hoped to do, and it proved to be a costly mistake, the expense of running it causing me to lose most of my money. I had not understood the difficulties I might face because of my desire to be a teacher, with all the responsibilities of giving tuition. But, I must say that Hastings gave me a fair quota of valuable experience, and so not all was lost.

The circumstances that led up to my leaving Hastings are perhaps what most readily come to mind when I think of how the Spirit worked while I was in that large house. The events began when the younger of my two daughters asked if she could stay with me for a while to have her first baby. She and her husband had been unable to find a home since he was transferred down south from his RAF base in Scotland.

They arrived at my house with their dog about a fortnight before Christmas. It was after only a day or so when the baby, a girl, was born. The arrival of this little one added much to the festive feeling.

Dear Chang, my discarnate companion and teacher, dropped a bit of a bombshell at Christmas, saying that I would have to move because of the difficulties in maintaining the house. What is more, he said that Maggie and I would move on January 27th, which seemed to be impossibly near, especially considering the fact that, apart from ourselves, my daughter and her husband had nowhere to go with their new child.

I had had enough experience to know that Chang's words would be proved correct, but my daughter and her husband were at a loss to know where to look for a home. Chang took a hand, saying, "When passing the houses just before reaching the airfield, you will feel drawn to a house. Knock upon the door. You will be made welcome when you speak of what you need."

And so it happened. On the way to the airfield where my son-in-law worked, he took note of his feelings as he passed the row of houses that had been spoken of. The last house reached had to be the one, for he felt no drawing power up till then. He knocked as he had been told to do, and a pleasant lady came to the door. He enquired if she had, by any chance, a flat or rooms to let. Hearing this request, the amazed lady said, "But how did you know? The place hasn't been advertised yet!"

Everything was agreed there and then, and the happy couple settled themselves at last. Their new home was more than comfortable, and the baby and the dog were greatly welcomed by the landlady. Chang was blessed by us all for his foresight.

Maggie and I then had the task of finding somewhere suitable for ourselves. Chang indicated that we should not stay in Hastings, for I had been drawn into a charitable group there and its members were taking advantage of me, making too many demands upon my time and my rapidly dwindling finances. He said that if I moved from the area it would be an honourable way out of a delicate situation. Apart from that, it was in any case time to move on to a new area and to new things.

25. ANCHOR VILLA

The time spent in Hastings had been a great financial drain upon me, and I knew that after selling my house and settling my debts I would not have sufficient money left to buy a property. So, Maggie and I had to look for somewhere to rent. We decided to begin our search in Dover, because I felt that the castle Len had shown me still bore some relevance. Dover was the only place other than Hastings where I knew there to be a castle on a hill, well above the promenade, much as I had seen with Len in the dream.

Both Maggie and I had visions wherein each saw a part of the picture, and from what was seen we had some idea of what to expect. We knew, for example, there would be a large flat we would like but that it would be taken. We also knew that work would be commenced more fully than before, but we were not advised as to what this might entail, free will ever having to be honoured.

In Dover we made enquiries at numerous estate agents' offices and were laughed at for asking about rented accommodation, such property rarely being available. We were almost giving up the search when we saw another house agent down a side street. We thought we may as well try there, and how glad we were that we did. We were told that there were, as our visions had foretold, three places vacant, and we were taken to view them there and then.

We saw firstly a terraced house, and that was too small, just as vision had led us to expect. Next came the large flat. This had been seen by a gentleman with a large family but he had not secured it. We very much liked the place and said that we would take it. Just at that moment, the man who had viewed it before us came rushing in.

"I was first," he exclaimed, "and I want it!"

We felt it only fair to give way.

The last of the three properties was in the village of St Margaret's at Cliffe, two or three miles from Dover. As far as this dwelling was concerned I had an idea what to expect, because I had heard a voice say, "There will be a house standing in its own grounds." On turning a corner into a lane in St Margaret's, Maggie and I saw a white house with small bay windows, standing by itself opposite a row of small cottages.

Margaret exclaimed, "This is it – this is the one I saw in vision! The windows were all blue, shining with the colour."

The blue seen by my friend told me that the work would go on there. This was the place for us, and we moved from Hastings on January 27th just as Chang said we would.

The house was indeed a place that held many possibilities for us to change much of what we had been doing. Having been told I should teach I was impatient to start, and made the mistake of being drawn into the local spiritualist church. I was encouraged by certain people to take responsibility in the church – until, that is, I learned that tuition was limited under such conditions.

But I get ahead of myself. Once we had moved into the white house, Anchor Villa, we soon made ourselves comfortable. It is not always known as to the suitability of a place in which one may think to be happy, the emotions of those concerned playing a particular part in laying the mental foundation upon which the happiness must grow.

The first night in Anchor Villa was to be an eventful time. Being tired I fell quickly asleep, only to be awakened by undue noise. I had no time to get out of bed to investigate, for, as my eyes opened, I found that I was level with and looking at a wooden leg, its companion leg having on it a long sea boot. My eyes travelled up the body and I almost froze in the bed – the visitor was a pirate. He had a black patch over one eye and a hat with a colourful knotted scarf under it, a lamp outside giving enough light by which to see.

"My name is John Smith," he said, his voice as loud as his clothing. "See that you do not let any of your women lie with my men. If any of you do, I will have you whipped!"

I almost laughed. "Why should we want to do that? None of us are likely to want such company."

"I'm warning you," he said. "I'll be back if I find out." And with that he was gone. There was not a sound in the house. It always seems impossible to me that only I myself hear these things.

The next day proved very interesting. I had to get food and went to the village store. There I found a number of women chatting together; I was the point of their discussion. On entering the shop all eyes turned toward me, taking in every bit of my appearance. They all knew I had taken the house that was known to be haunted. I introduced myself to them and moved toward the counter.

"What can I do for you?" the assistant said. He was very affable.

"Did you sleep last night?" said one lady, showing a tendency to be nervous.

"Oh yes," I said. "But I saw the pirate and he threatened me."

There was an exclamation as I spoke. "You've *seen* him?" the same lady said.

For some reason, no one seemed able to believe that I had actually seen him. "What's he like?" queried one of the others.

I answered, explaining what I had seen and adding that his name was John Smith. "That's right," said the man behind the counter. "I know where you can borrow a book which tells of everything he did in this village."

I took the address of the elderly lady who owned the book and promised to let them know the result.

The lady was a kind old soul, more than willing to let me see the book. On the first page was a picture of the man I had seen. His exploits were many, including the whipping of three or four young women and leaving them in the churchyard, tied to a tree. Realising what a nasty piece of work he was, I thought I had better seek help, and so I spoke to Chang about him. I am not sure what was done, but I neither saw nor heard any more of the pirate.

I thought that might be the end of my discarnate visitors, but I was wrong. The next night a very irate elderly lady came to me. She had been the district nurse and was my predecessor at Anchor Villa, where she had lived for many years. At eighty she became housebound; at ninety she had died. Winnie, an old friend of hers and one of my neighbours, had told me about her when she came to welcome Maggie and me.

The old woman's somewhat thin voice was given volume by her anger at my presence as she shouted, "Get out. We don't want your kind here."

I was shocked, for this was somewhat unexpected. I replied, "I know you can make it very uncomfortable for us here, but what would your friend Winnie have to say about that?"

"Winnie?" she said, aghast that I should mention the lady who had already adhered herself to us since we had moved in.

"Yes, Winnie," I said. "I shall tell her, you know. She thinks you were kind and loving."

The old lady was flustered. "Don't tell her. Tell her I loved her and was so grateful for all she did."

"Winnie is now better in health," I said. "The pressure of mind you put upon her made her ill."

"What do you mean?" she retorted. "I made her comfortable and gave her food."

"It is the mind that puts pressure on," I said. "You did not like her to go home, and that put her in a difficult position because she had a family."

"My Winnie," she said, shaken at the thought of what had been done. "Please tell her I am happy to have had a chance to speak to someone. I haven't spoken to anyone else since I passed on. I could not make people listen; they all feared this place."

"I don't wonder," was all I said. "You are the second one to threaten me since we took up residence!" The idea of exorcism came to me, but then I said to myself, "No, that won't do."

The elderly lady knew what I had in mind and said, "Don't do that, please. I don't know where I should go."

I said, "That could very soon be settled. You have a friend whom you chose not to marry because you were so tied up with your career as a nurse. He is now free and will take you to the cottage that has been waiting a long time for you."

Her eyes opened wide. "I always wanted a cottage," she said. "Do you mean it would belong to me?"

"There is no need to hold on to anything, for no

one will take it away and no one will enter if not of the same mind as yourself. When he comes for you, go happily and don't look back at the past."

It was not long when we had another visit from the old woman. She said she had gone with her friend and had returned just to thank us for what we had done, and to ask us to give Winnie her love.

It was during our time at Anchor Villa that I wrote my first book, *And Some Have Mansions*, a novel about a coach crash and the experiences of the various victims and survivors. Although the story itself is fiction, it is based upon things I have seen in my research into the background of daily life. The writing of this book was, I feel, one of the main things to come out of the time spent at that house.

26. MAGGIE

The idea of moving from Anchor Villa began as a thought to make life easier for Maggie. I should explain that I first met her at my centre in London. She came to see me because she had cancer of the womb and it was feared that her legs would have to be amputated. Through the power of love she was healed over two days, and her joy was such that she wanted to learn more. From then on she remained a good and constant friend. Unfortunately, though, while at St Margaret's, Maggie was found once again to have cancer; this time it was leukaemia. Even so, bless her, she insisted on helping as much as she was able. Her mediumship was a joy to her and she soldiered on, giving comfort to others where she could.

One could ask, "Why couldn't she be healed again?" And the simple answer is that she wanted to die. The man whom she loved was waiting for her, and she found the responsibilities of the material life to be a constant worry. So, quite simply, she had resigned herself to passing over. Healing could therefore only ease her discomfort, and she was content with that.

Despite her courage, Maggie found that living at St Margaret's added to her burden, for much that was part of her life involved trips to Dover, either to go to the doctor or to carry on her work at the spiritualist church. So it was that, with her comfort in mind, I prayed for a place in Dover so she might be saved the travelling to and from the town. I knew that my prayer had been heard, for I had a dream in which we were quickly ushered out of Anchor Villa's front door by Uida, a loving Arab who worked with Chang. We now had only to wait and see how my request would be granted.

Granted it was indeed, and in the way usually associated with the method of the light – one thing leading to another. In the spiritualist church in Dover, a small band of ladies and I were down to give healing. We were able to give help to a number of people, despite the efforts of one person whose aim was to discredit us. One night after the healing had finished I noticed a number of women had remained behind talking together. A state of excitement seemed to ooze from them.

"I like your new healer," one of them said to me, smiling knowingly. "Introduce him to us, won't you?"

I was surprised. "*Him*?" I said. "We don't have a man helping us."

She looked at me, smiling as if she did not believe me. The church lights were put out and we left the building, locking the door behind us.

"Where is your man friend?" I was asked by another of the women.

"What man?" I replied, astonished at being asked

a second time.

"The one doing the healing with you," she replied. "You know – he came and washed his hands as you all did after each healing."

"There was no man with us," I had to say. I was sorry to disappoint her, but she and the other women became more elated when realising that the man who had been giving healing to them was someone passed over and not of the earth!

As we moved towards the bus stop, another lady left those she had been walking with and commenced talking to me.

"I didn't want to talk in front of the others," she said, "but I understand you want to leave St Margaret's and move into Dover. Is that right?"

"I would be pleased if I could get nearer," I said. "The journey is rather too much for Maggie, and the fares are crippling us coming to the church almost every day. I didn't know I was letting myself in for this when I was asked to back the new church president. She'd said, 'I won't take on the presidency unless Mrs Franklin can be vice-president.' And that's how it started."

We stood still for a moment, and I pointed to a nearby house that had a very nice balcony on the middle of its three floors.

"On Sunday I came past here with a friend who was staying the weekend," I said, "and as we passed this house I commented how lovely for Maggie if we could have a place like that, where she could sit on the balcony and enjoy looking over at the park."

The lady was so quiet that I wondered if I had said too much.

"But that is where I want to take you," she said after a long moment. "There is a flat available – the one with the balcony, in fact. What an amazing thing!"

"How glad I am you thought of me," I said. "I am so very grateful. It will make such a difference to be near the church."

"It is my sister's flat," explained the lady, "but her husband passed away recently and she doesn't want to stay there. She left on the day he died and hasn't been back. Now everything is being removed but the carpets. I have the key. Would you like to go in with me and look around?"

The place was everything I had thought, and I was very pleased to say yes to taking it on.

"My sister wants fifty pounds for the carpets," said the lady. "Could you manage that?"

Promptly I said I would. I didn't stop to think how I would afford the move and all it would entail. Nor did I for a moment consider how I would become free of Anchor Villa, the lease of which would not expire for another eighteen months. Filled with excitement, I thanked the lady for her most valuable help, said goodbye and went to catch my bus home.

That night, after talking it over with Maggie, I went to bed, very thankful for the blessing being given to me. I was overjoyed and relieved as I thought of how much less the rent would be, and how large and comfortable the flat was. And to think that it had such a wonderful balcony too.

Contented with the day I soon fell asleep, only to be awakened by the faint form of someone standing by my bed. Smiling, an elderly gentleman showed himself more clearly and said, "I died so that you could have the flat."

"What about your wife?" I gasped. I could not understand his desire to give up his life.

"She was no real wife," he said. "We didn't have much in common. I knew when I dug the small garden that the effort would see me off, but I did it gladly." And with that he was gone.

I remember thinking what a blessing it was that this man had happily laid down his life to help us on our way. Everything seemed to be working in our favour. No wonder that, when the time came, the agent allowed us to take the flat even though there were twenty-five people in front of us on the short list – a miracle indeed!

The next step was to free ourselves from the lease to Anchor Villa, and I did not know quite how this would be managed. I soon had the answer to that problem. Village life hides nothing, and it was when I went to the shop for our groceries that I found out this held true in our neighbourhood.

"Do you know your house is up for sale?" a woman asked me. She was breathless as she passed on the news.

I smiled. I did not have to say what had happened to me; I just had to have courage to see things through. Without going back to the house I went to see the owner of the property, asking him if what I had been told was correct. He said it was but that I was not to worry, for the sale was being put through with us as sitting tenants.

"But wouldn't you prefer to sell it without tenants?" I enquired.

"I hadn't thought about it," he said. "You'd never be able to find anywhere to go in time."

"Give me a fortnight," I replied. "I am sure I can be away from the house by then."

Thankfully, there were no bothersome intruders to hinder the sale, and I knew that Anchor Villa would now be a happier house for anyone who moved into it. I felt confident that the flat could be ready in the time allotted.

All was ready in a week. The papers signed, we moved in within the fourteen days mentioned. We were elated. A friend, with whom I still correspond today, was a magnificent help. She took us in her car so we could be at the flat prior to the arrival of the furniture van. Once all was in place we couldn't have been happier. The light of life had done it yet again.

One day, quite some time after Maggie and I had become settled in our flat, I was called to the spiritualist church and accused of something I did not do. This was rather a blow to me, for I had given all I could in both time and money, and my health had become less than good. Being tired of the constant call on my time, I was very ready to comply with the command to leave the church. Besides, I knew that the way was being made for another phase of my life to begin.

My treasured Maggie was losing strength, so I took her to stay with an old friend, Dinah, who lived in Hastings and was very dear to us. Chang had promised me that Maggie would pass over peacefully without being put in hospital, and Dinah, a retired nurse, had offered to care for her. There she would be safe from being pestered by a woman in Dover who was proving to be a great nuisance to the tired and ailing Maggie.

In Hastings, Maggie had three wonderful days of loving care and attention. Friends queued outside the house to take a turn at talking to her. On the third day, after the evening meal – which she could not eat because of her lack of appetite – she passed quietly away.

Dinah said afterwards, "I have seen many people who are dying, and there is usually something that shows they are on their way out, but I could not see it with Maggie."

27. GILLINGHAM

With the death of Maggie I lost a very close friend but knew I must get ready for the time in front of me. Through a contact of mine I was able to secure a rented house in Gillingham, very near to Chatham Docks. I moved there with Eleanor, whom I had met in Dover. She had recently retired from working as a matron at a school for sons of servicemen, and said she would like to go with me.

Life had many ups and downs. Trying to teach was indeed hard, as I was told it would be. It seemed that people could not grasp the real use of the inward self; it was so much easier for them to lean on the goodness of someone who died pinned to a cross.

All through my working life my joy has been research, especially time spent out of the body. The inner self has led me to some lovely places, but I have also had to see the lower planes – where the astral self must take the brunt of all that is done in the earth in contradiction of the natural laws.

Knowledge and loving friends have I found, but in Gillingham there was one young woman I had come to trust who put me in danger. Out of the condition came a thrill I have never forgotten. There was a class once a week that she had joined. Suddenly she stopped coming and I wondered as to whether I should ring up to find out if she was sick. On the third week of her absence I telephoned her home and her husband said, "I'm afraid my wife has gone to class and has not yet returned."

"That is why I rang," I said. "She was not at class and I wondered if she had been taken ill. She has been away three weeks."

The husband said, "I'm sorry to hear about that."

I just thanked him and said goodbye, hoping his wife would ring me the next day.

During the night I had a very vivid and exciting dream. I found myself – in sleep – taking a short cut through a park. A young man came running toward me, brandishing a bottle. Before he could strike me, strong arms lifted me up and I flew through the air. The running man threw the bottle, but it went below my feet. A chuckle burst from the two men carrying me, and one said with a laugh in his voice, "Missed!"

They put me down on a very light thoroughfare and said, "You'll be all right now."

We were by an underground station and I thought it would be safer to go home by train. I did not remember getting on a train but woke up in the safety of my bed, wondering what all that was about.

I was not left long in doubt, for the young woman rang me and was somewhat annoyed I had phoned her husband. I said I had no wish to pry, and that had she rung me and told me she was leaving I should have understood and would not have phoned.

"I was out with the taxi driver," she said. "He is very angry that I cannot see him any more, because my husband will no longer trust me to go out."

I then related my dream, and explained that a man who will kill for what he wants (the taxi driver as shown in the dream) would not for long be a good companion; he could become very demanding. A little later I had a visit from her. She was happy and said, "My husband and I have found a better understanding. I am now so glad you phoned and showed me what might have happened."

I was very pleased to hear the outcome of her indiscretion and felt she would never trespass again on the trust of people.

At that time I myself could have distrusted people, and there were many happenings that could have broken my faith. Nine people started a new class with me, and for three weeks everyone appeared to be enthusiastic. But on the night of the fourth week's class no one came, except one gentleman who said he would be leaving the group. I discovered that a medium who had joined the class had told all the students that she could teach them much better, and in believing her, all had gone to her. Only the one man was leaving for another reason, which was that his wife was returning to him after a period of absence.

I was sad for them all, for I inwardly knew that the medium would encourage a reliance upon spirits which would not give them the ability to fully bless other people, or leave them with anything to feed their inward selves. The progress of the self is all-important, but the brain can often be turned away from a progressive path. Once the joy of true love is found, however, there is nothing that can at any time take its place.

◆ ◆ ◆

Eleanor and I realised the time was drawing near to us having to leave the house we had made very comfortable, for we needed sufficient rooms to house those who wanted to study under our roof.

One particular day stands out, which made us hurry into making arrangements, although we were totally unaware of the event at the time it happened. Eleanor and I had finished all we had to do for the day and went into the lounge. Our lights were on and the curtains were open, but it was not until afterwards that we found out a group of people had been gawping at us through the large front windows. Perhaps we did not see them because we were sat glued to a film on television. Nothing out of the ordinary it would seem. However, it was the next day when cleaning the tiled front porch that I heard a group of people pointedly whispering to one another as they passed the house.

Then a woman shouted at me, "Witch!"

I was flabbergasted. My calling had not previously caused such a reaction; those living near us had talked with me, and none had seemed antagonistic.

"Why do you say that?" I called after the woman.

"You're the only one in town that had light last night," she said, anger causing her voice to sound vengeful. "We all had to light candles," she continued, and with head in the air she moved on, the others following.

I went inside quickly, not really understanding the situation. On ringing up friends I was informed that a blackout had put the town in darkness; only the hospital had light. Eleanor and I thought great blessing had been given us. We often worked into the night to send off literature, and we accepted the miracle with gladness. It did not worry me unduly, feeling the situation with the locals would pass, but from that time on my neighbours were very wary of me. This, then, spurred on the idea of moving.

Over lunch, Eleanor and I discussed a move. One of our students had offered us two floors and a basement in a house she owned near to the main thoroughfare in Gillingham, and we agreed the location would give us added opportunity where the work was concerned. Buses and trains were quite handy, which made the place accessible. We made the arrangement to look the place over.

One gentleman had been in the property and he was aged, so not a lot had been done as far as upkeep was concerned. When we looked it over we could see some work was needed to make it habitable. After settling all the conditions of our renting the accommodation, which was furnished, we commenced our packing and preparation for moving.

I had had no news from the spirit world and thought all was well, forgetting that our free will cannot be tampered with by those who value progress. We can, however, be waylaid by lesser ones, whose encouragement through one of the earth may force us to break faith with the things we love best, labelling us as unfaithful and perhaps untrustworthy.

The house we had come from, lovely as it was, had been costly to run; I had needed to work hard to keep it going. Nevertheless, we somewhat regretted our move when seeing exactly all that had to be done in our new place. Our student who owned the property explained that she was not in a position to help us, but with the aid of good friends we gradually replaced threadbare carpets and rickety furniture until all was very comfortable. It was only then that I began to have dreams of difficulties, though in not seeing their origin I just had to hope we could avoid any mishap.

28. A STING IN THE TAIL

After a while the younger students who had taken up residence with us wanted to practise their public speaking ability. I conceived the idea of taking them to Speakers' Corner in Hyde Park, where, with the aid of a soap box, free speech could be practised. Each Sunday morning found us on the road to London. Encouragement had to be kept up in this, for there was pressure from all sides as different religions tried to blight the ardour of the young people. It says much for them that we often had the largest crowd about our stand, and from this were put into action ideas of commencing a class in London.

We all enjoyed the experience of talking in Hyde Park. The practice it gave was very valuable, and soon the students were considered ready to serve the churches in and around London. Once visiting a church they were booked again, and much regret was ours when having to break with the majority of that work, but the car we had was not really fit for journeys to and from London. We decided to get another vehicle, and so perused the advertisements for something suitable to our purpose.

At last we felt we had seen the right one. It was being sold by a man who had broken his leg, could no longer drive, and apparently needed the money.

We liked the sound of his voice when phoning for details, and an appointment to view the vehicle was made. Being delighted with the car we paid for it there and then, looking forward to being able to resume our longer journeys. But there lay in store a disappointment that I did not anticipate; I had relied on my brain and had not given my inward self the opportunity to say whether or not the purchase was worthwhile.

Being sensitive to activity when asleep, I heard someone coming up the stairs. In my sleep I saw the man from whom we had bought the car; he was climbing the stairs two at a time. He had a large wrench in his hand as he came into my room. Seeing me ostensibly asleep, he said, "Good!" and then left, hurrying downstairs with no sign of a broken leg.

When we wanted to use the car the next morning it would not start. From a nearby garage a man came to look at it.

"What a mess," he said. "We shall have to take it in."

"But it went beautifully yesterday," I ventured to say.

"That was yesterday," he replied. "It wouldn't go today."

The car was towed in and gone were our journeys. We were held up for about two months over that, the garage mechanic being rather unhelpful. No matter how often we spoke to him, there always seemed to be an excuse for his not having finished the repairs.

I had not wanted to seek help from the class, but when we gathered together I told them about it to see if anything could be done. After I had spoken, one of the students, a young policeman, spoke up.

"I couldn't repair a car," he said, "but I could go to see the mechanic and find out why he is taking so long without giving you a valid reason."

I was very grateful for this and accepted his offer. When he arrived to take me to the garage he looked very authoritative in his uniform, which, with his being very tall, he wore to perfection.

Once we were inside the garage the mechanic looked disturbed.

He said, "I don't know about that car. Every time I go to do it, something happens and I have to hurry away and leave it. I'd be glad to be rid of it. It's not good for us to leave a car unrepaired. Frankly, I wouldn't mind it being taken away."

That same day, the car was towed away from the garage and left outside our house. Another man came to look at it.

"It is only a small job," he said. "Someone has loosened all the wires."

When told of this, the man who had sold us the car laughed. "I said you should bring it back if you found it wouldn't go."

Perhaps I would have done just that, but Chang informed me that no money would be returned if

I did. It seemed that the fellow used his injury as a means of playing upon people's sympathy. He had apparently had the car returned more than once. Soft-hearted individuals had listened to his sob story that he could not afford to return their money, and fearing expensive repairs they had left the car with him. Because we had been made aware of this and had kept the vehicle, we stopped a very lucrative racket. In any case, once repaired the car went perfectly and travelling once more became a sheer joy to us.

The next step for us was to begin teaching in London. Advertisements helped to gather a small but very sincere group, and after booking a room in Caxton Hall we commenced the class. As students they found the philosophy to be a very practical foundation for everyday living.

The classes there gave us all great pleasure. In fact a few of the students enjoyed learning so much that when we eventually ceased going to Caxton Hall, they travelled from London to Gillingham each week to attend a class. Supper after the class was always a happy affair, the resident students making sure the visitors had all they needed. The visiting students would then spend the night as our guests and go to work in London the next day.

A young man joined our weekly class, saying he needed tuition. After the first week it was realised that all was not well with him. At class the following week he was questioned but evaded answering. When at last I saw a spirit with him he said that was why he had come. This 'helper', as he called it, was not a good one, but gave him what he thought was good clairvoyance. The young man wanted me to exorcise this helper without losing the clairvoyance it gave him. I had to tell him it was impossible to do as he asked.

The next night, we – the resident students, Eleanor and I – were late finishing for the day. We were about to go to bed when one of the students went downstairs and found the front door enveloped in flames. The emergency services were notified immediately. Thankfully, our young people soon had the fire out, opening windows to get rid of the unpleasant smell of smoke. A fire engine and a police car were with us in minutes, the firemen and the police officers only too pleased to see the danger already over. After making sure the fire was fully out they joined us for coffee and biscuits, the evening ending on a happy note despite the seriousness of the event.

Investigation by the police rapidly brought forward witnesses who had seen the fire started by a young man – the same one to whom we had spoken at the class on the night before the arson attack. He was arrested and eventually tried and convicted. The landlady did well out of the insurance, and so no one suffered. Except, of course, the young man, who brought upon himself ill from which we would gladly have shielded him had he given us the opportunity.

In those days I did not always try to discern; I accepted people when they appeared to me to be sincere. But I then learnt to think differently and to ask when I was not sure of anyone. This lesson was courtesy of a young man whom I took in as a resident student because he said he wanted to learn but had nowhere to stay. Without asking for references I allowed him to use the comfortable basement room. He brought with him some furniture and some other belongings.

My birthday was several weeks after the young man's arrival, and what a birthday it turned out to be. We all went to a medieval dinner at a castle in Kent. It was a lovely evening, and we were all still talking about it effusively when we arrived back at the house late that night.

Our new resident young man produced a present for me and quite openly said, "I took the money for it out of the cash box."

The cash box was empty when I looked. "What am I going to feed you all on?" I asked, completely dumbfounded. "I do not get money easily."

The conversation that followed revealed that he had been taking pocket money from the box for some weeks. As I trusted everyone it had not occurred to me to count the contents. The young man boasted that when he and his wife were going through their divorce proceedings he had been able to take for himself all the best furniture.

"I said I had given it all to charity," he said gleefully.

"And so you will," I answered. "Tomorrow our basement will be cleared and you with it."

"Why?" he asked as if he were innocent.

"Because I cannot trust you. No one takes the petty cash. It is irresponsible and unfair to everyone else."

He tried unsuccessfully to get his things removed himself, but a charity I had phoned came and collected them. "Speak the truth in future," I told him. "No one will trust you or want you if you don't."

I found out that he had been drinking heavily in his room before going to bed, accounting for the fact I had rarely seen him in the latter part of the evening. I could have been truly bowled over, but I was very glad that I was made stronger so as to cope with the situation.

He did not go immediately; he said he had nowhere to go. I was emphatic that he should leave as soon as possible. It was at this time that I had a disturbing dream of being in a darkened place where there were animal cages, each containing either a lion, a tiger, or a monkey. There were other people with me who were somewhat afraid of the animals. The dream ended with me encouraging many of those people to follow me into a much lighter place.

I knew this dream meant further trouble, that

lions and tigers symbolise certain solicitors and lawyers, and monkeys represent people who make mischief. I wondered whether the young man and his lingering with us would be the cause of it, but it turned out that another blow to my faith in human nature was soon to be struck by a completely unexpected assailant.

29. ADRIFT ON A RAFT

The young man did finally leave, and for a while we managed to gain a feeling of quiet and purpose which enabled us to continue our work. This did not last long, however. The landlady quite suddenly ceased to be interested in our work and began to be desirous of our leaving her property. She made her feelings known, and the fact that she had turned against us for no apparent reason shook me greatly, so much so that I began to wonder how trustworthy people really were.

Having had the dream of the wild animals, I was not surprised when she said I would be hearing from her solicitors. I explained to her that I should be happy to leave as soon as I could arrange alternative accommodation, but she apparently wanted us out of there so quickly that she tried to obtain a legal order to force us to quit immediately. I knew that whatever I was about to undergo would add to my understanding, but such matters were still disturbing to me, and I was concerned as to how or where I would find a suitable place for all of us.

Two nights before the court hearing I had a further dream in which I found myself at the front gate of the house. As I stood looking across the road a great crevasse opened up in front of me. Looking down into it I felt the need to jump over before the gap became too wide. I woke from that dream somewhat uneasy but soon fell asleep again. The experience continued, but this time I was on the other side of the crevasse, and I was able to step onto a bus that had drawn silently up to the kerb.

This dream told me that my inner self had been busy enlisting the aid of sincere loved ones who, though passed from the earth, could still help. I was greatly cheered by the content of the experience, for it indicated that I would successfully get over the crisis represented by the crevasse. The bus symbolised a class, assuring me that no matter what was about to happen somewhere would be found where classes would once again commence.

Waking the next morning was a pleasure. I knew help could be found and I trusted in that. It was the day before I had to go to the court, and quite understandably I felt a little uncomfortable as evening arrived. However, I told myself it was not the end and renewed my trust in what I had seen.

There was nothing too disturbing at the hearing, except having to leave behind everything I had bought to make the place clean and habitable. On the plus side, though, the landlady's plan to see us off quickly somewhat backfired, for the court gave us three months in which to vacate the premises. Thinking things over, I was thankful that my plight was not so bad as those who had no loving ones to give them mental comfort and love. I remembered my dream of getting away from the caged animals. I now knew what it was like to be at the receiving end of legal action, but I also understood how it was possible to deal with such matters in a positive way. From now on I would indeed be able to assist others in a similar predicament.

Although so far we had nowhere to move to, I encouraged the students to start packing china and so on. Literature was prepared in advance so that there would be no rush when we managed to get somewhere to reside. The crevasse was opening as our peace was disturbed and our money made short, and I wondered what might yet be possible to help us back on our feet.

After a heavy day, I was meditating in a chair when suddenly I found myself aboard ship. At first it was a very lovely feeling watching the wake of the moving vessel, but suddenly there was a loud crash. A life raft was thrown onto the sea at the side of the ship.

"Jump!" someone shouted. "The ship is sinking."

I jumped and landed on the raft. Without paddle or motor the raft turned and headed for land. Somehow I knew it would take me safely to the shore. It was clear from this that help would be provided in our hour of need.

◆ ◆ ◆

One of the students had friends living in Ramsgate.

They were kind and loving people, and in response to a phone call they offered to house some of our number until we found a place suitable for us all. We accepted the offer gladly, but their home could not accommodate our work and much had to come to a stop. I consoled everyone by reminding them of the dream in which I saw myself getting aboard a bus, and that meant that classes would soon be under way again. "Don't worry," I told them. "We shall have a place, of that I am sure."

Each day I bought a newspaper to look at the advertisements. But it was a few weeks before, tucked away in the corner of a page in a newspaper, there was an advertisement for a house to rent not far from Canterbury.

A dream followed the excitement of seeing the advertisement, but I was somewhat bewildered by it. I fell into a deep sleep as soon as I went to bed; it seemed I was awake as I was aware of what was happening. I was in the company of an elderly man. He was hurrying me to get a job finished. We were on a bridge, and the top of a wall that edged the bridge had to be polished. I had covered most of it when suddenly the man clutched my arm. "Hurry, hurry!" he almost screamed. When I looked around I could see two men coming onto the bridge. "There will be nothing left if they catch us," the elderly man said, almost weeping with his desire to be away. How I finished the work I do not know, but I was away before the men reached the spot. The old man had completely disappeared, and I must have done the same by waking up in my bed.

It lightened the moment as I retold the experience, and everyone thought it was to do with a speedy move. I thought, 'Oh, to speak with Chang,' who had often unravelled bewildering sleepstates for me. I needed but the thought and Chang was there on the instant; he knew that I would not call unless needing urgent advice. I explained to him my experience.

"This dream is very important to you," he said quietly. "The bridge is the work, and some preparation has to be done to get things moving again. If certain people should get rid of you in your sleep, all our work would come to a standstill. There are those who covet darkness; to them the light is abhorrent. They cannot live where light prevails. You give off light, and there are many who do not like it because it shows up their bad traits of character. They will destroy that light if it is at all possible.

"The man helping you in the dream is a watchman, and he is working out his retribution."

"He was very nervous," I said, hoping Chang would say more.

"I have no doubt he was," came Chang's reply. "He'd been thieving for the other two men, who took most of what he gained from his profitable nightly work. Their greed helped him to make up his mind to break free from taking what was not his. The moment he stopped stealing for them they beat him up in the earth life and he died. The two men are much more of a menace than the old man who has since regretted his actions. He is now willing to help us in order to repay his debt to the sincere, and thereby he will bring benefit to those he previously stole from. It is much better for him to do this than to suffer further at the hands of those men."

Getting back to the accommodation problem, I thought at first that the advertised house might be too expensive, and then I remembered the encouragement I had received. I phoned the agents to arrange a viewing. I felt a certain sense of mild urgency, for we could see difficulties starting to arise by prolonging our stay in Ramsgate.

On going to my bed that night it was not easy to relax for sleep, but just before I dozed off I heard a man's voice near at hand. "So we meet again," he said.

I looked to see who it was and immediately recognised the Man in Grey. He greeted me with a smile, but he was very serious when he asked, "Would you prefer a large house or a small one?"

I looked steadily at him. It was of the young people that I was thinking and I said, "The large one would be best, for a small one would not have enough rooms."

He looked at me as if I had taken leave of my senses, but, again smiling at me, he said, "So be it."

There was more yet I had to learn. In making my choice, one period had ended and a new one started. We were able to go into the big property I had seen advertised, unknowing, however, of what an alternative, smaller place might have produced in terms of the work for the Spirit.

30. THE HOUSE IN THE COUNTRY

The house was an old property full of character, set in the country a few miles outside Canterbury. Unfortunately, the state of both house and furnishings was not good, but allowance in the advance rent we paid was made by the landlord for the repairs that we had to do to make the place homely and comfortable. Mould was on split and torn covers on settees and chairs. Thankfully, it was high summer and most of the furniture could be put outside to dry once washed thoroughly. Doors and windows were left open all day as we cleaned and polished, glued broken furniture and re-covered the seats whose covers were well beyond cleaning. Any hopelessly damaged furniture was put away in the loft.

With all of the live-in students taking up rooms, there was relatively little available space left for us to help ourselves financially by taking in paying guests. However, the rather high cost of keeping the place going was covered by two of the resident students taking jobs. Another student of our work gave us a substantial weekly donation for which we blessed him then and still do today. The large garden could have been a problem, but wide grassy lawns, flower beds and fruit trees made it a wonderful treasure to us, with plenty of space to start a vegetable garden. I felt blessed and much rested by the good air, but I soon learned my first lesson at that house – too much time given to the bodily cares of people slowed up the work of the soul, and I needed this to come first. From that point on we endeavoured to go back to putting our full effort into answering letters, printing and sending out literature, and running classes.

One morning I was up early as usual but started to feel dizzy, and found dazzling flashes coming across my eyes. I called for help. Chang came and spoke with me, telling me to take two days in bed and I would be well. I told my students and they unanimously said, "We will do everything. Do not worry."

Gladly I went to lie down, but a noise roused me to look around the room. The noise came from an elderly lady sitting up in the other, spare bed. She was very agitated.

"What are you doing in bed?" she demanded. "I want my lunch!"

For a moment I couldn't speak; my head didn't seem to be mine. But suddenly a thought came to me and I said, "I'm doing no cooking today. If you want a meal, you go and get it."

"I can't do that!" she exclaimed, waving her fist at me, thinking she could force me.

However, before she could say anything more I said, "There are others doing the cooking today, so go and ask."

"No," she said. "I have asked before and you are the only one that will look after me."

I thought to myself, 'No wonder my sleep is disturbed. I shall have to do something with her.' She did not move, and I said, quite positively, "Why don't you go where you can get what you want. I am certainly not going to get up for you."

She hissed at me, but went from her bed to my wardrobe and took from it clothing I had never seen before and also an old and battered case. Having pushed into the case a few other things, she put on an old-fashioned hat and coat. She then went out.

I saw no more of her and I was glad; her using me during the night-time had obviously been playing its part in my sickness. Everyone needs to get in sleep to where it is colourful in the worlds unseen, for the time of sleep is when it is possible for the inward self to be fed.

My next experience worried me somewhat as it concerned the landlord's daughter, whom I saw in a dream as a baby in a pram. Upon the baby's face a cat had fallen asleep, and the child was dead. In the dream I then met an elderly lady who had been the child's nanny when it was in the earth plane. Apparently, the child's father had so mourned the loss of his baby that he had drawn both the child and the lady – now passed from the earth – back to this house.

"Please write to him," the old lady pleaded. "I am

tired. I want to go and rest, for the child wears me out." She looked at the child, whom I could now see as an infant running round the trees, full of life.

The owner had made it very clear he wanted no correspondence from me and that the agents must not allow me to send on a letter. I therefore did what I could to exorcise the lady and the child so that they might find a happier way of life. I do not know the full results of my efforts, but I saw neither the girl nor the lady again.

◆ ◆ ◆

Some weeks later it was the twenty-first birthday of one of my grandchildren, and a party was duly arranged. Any get-together of our family was a big affair as many members of the clan usually attended, and the numbers were boosted further by friends and neighbours. The party was very lively, music and dance being enjoyed to the full. I had not been dancing for many years as I suffered from pain in my legs. When I was asked to dance, I thought I had better show willing. I enjoyed the experience and was not seated all the rest of the evening.

It was three o'clock in the morning when we arrived home. The night was half spent and I had to be up early in the morning. Relaxing, I sat on the side of my bed, thinking over the happy time we had had, although I began to wonder if I should have stayed on my feet dancing for so long a period.

Sitting on the side of my bed deep in thought, I did not see the door of my room open. The quiet movement of feet upon the carpet caught my eye and I looked up, expecting to see someone familiar. This, however, was not the case, for the visitor was a monk whom I had never seen before.

He had a bowl of steaming water in his hands and a soft, fluffy towel over his arm. After putting the bowl on the floor in front of me he took first one foot and then the other, placing them gently into the water. It was both soothing and comforting as he splashed the water up the side of my legs.

I felt somehow I did not warrant this attention, but I picked up the thought that my inner self deserved the much-needed help. Gently the monk dabbed each leg dry. He was, I remember, most careful with my toes. Getting up from his knees, he spoke one word, "Sleep." Picking up the bowl he smiled and went out of the room, closing the door after him. During the day that followed my few hours' sleep I felt no pain and thanked the loving one who had ministered to me in my need.

31. ACROSS THE WATER

Circumstances began to affect everyone as Eleanor sadly entered hospital, the cancer being too much for us to cope with. I was told I must go away for a while to regain my own health and to gain knowledge. Four of us toured England, briefly touching Scotland to go and see a gentleman who, it was thought, might aid us in moving forward with our philosophy. On the way back home we came through Leicester. Miss Hilda Watson, a lady I had previously met when serving one of the spiritualist churches in the city, run by a Mr Franey, had begged me to call and see her. We found her to be very sick. She was worrying about the church, of which she had been made Life President some time before.

I reminded her that I was a teacher and not desirous of being tied to a church. "Then why not teach in the church. We have never had a teacher before," she quickly said. I was undecided at first, but being pressed I accepted the responsibility. Returning home to Canterbury, we began to make plans for moving to the Midlands to be near the church.

Before we actually moved to Leicester, my dear Eleanor passed away. She had not wanted to move from Canterbury, but it was expedient for us to do so. And it was a dream that hastened me in my efforts to find a suitable house. The dream was very vivid. In it I was standing at the front door of the Canterbury house, looking over the garden. Suddenly a train came rushing round the side of the house. As it came nearer, the ground fell away and the train slid into a gaping hole. I gasped and then found myself awake and sitting up in bed, still startled.

Another dream on the same night showed me the inside of the church we were to take on. In one corner was a tree, and I saw myself hanging strings of pearls upon it. A voice I did not recognise spoke quickly, saying, "It is for a time that you will be here. Do the best you can; the rest shall not be your responsibility."

After talking of these things to my students we managed to find a house to rent, ten miles out of Leicester. It took time, effort and travel every day to carry the burden put upon us at the church, so before a year was up we moved again to another house within the city boundary.

We learned a great deal as we put time unstintingly to the church, but in many ways my decision to take on the responsibility of that place proved to be a serious mistake. In pleasing Miss Watson, the President, I displeased others, among them the church trustees. Human nature was revealed which bore out my original misgivings, for by underhand means I was forced to give up my work in the church, sick at heart with what had been said to me. It was unfortunately a time when quite a few innocent people found themselves caught in the fallout. And this I recognised as what was meant by my dream of the train falling into a hole. The train symbolised the help we had been able to give to many people while we were there, before they were tossed into the trap of ignorance, being waylaid by words spoken by the trustees that were not of the quality expected from supposed followers of the Light. How glad I was that I had learned not to grieve at what I myself lost. I was, however, very sad that friends I had made could no longer be with me.

The wonderful happening in the night after being made to leave was something I shall always remember, for the Master again stood at the foot of my bed and said, "And so persecuted they the prophets which were before me. They do not know that the poorest upon the earth can earn the crown of gold, and that no gem of the earth is valued as are the gems of tolerance, patience, mercy and kindness. I came to teach this to the people. The twos and threes seeking the way of love shall enter the light, but those who think they are of God may not be known in that capacity. Teach, my dear, and do not fear."

❖ ❖ ❖

Through the varying avenues of thought one can reach out and find the answer to many aspects of human nature. Time and mind is at a premium with the majority of people, but to those who give time freely, innate blessing can be found. All that is of oneself can automatically increase. Trusting in this I thought to go to Canada with one of my students, where for some time we had been invited to stay, to teach and make new friends.

This could not have happened without the support of mutual love. It so happened that though we had accepted the invitation we found ourselves short of funds, but a dream gave me new courage and trust was fully compensated. The night has ever been my period of strengthening, and I rejoiced at what the dream foretold. At first I was walking on the sea. Real life would never get me to try that, but in the dream it appeared quite natural. The waves were high but I walked on for some distance. I then found a concrete path in the midst of the sea; stepping on to it I walked steadily for a while until it dawned on me that the path commenced halfway to Canada. When I awoke realisation came to me that we would find one half of the air fare and the rest would be found from the people in Canada.

The next day I had a call from Canada. "You were with us last night," claimed an excited voice. "You were teaching us. We all know you will be over after that."

I then told our friends what Chang had said, that by Saturday we should know what was possible, and I would keep them updated. In my heart I knew all would be well and we would be able to travel.

Saturday came, and the post was wonderful. Cheques and postal orders were pouring in and we were able to go the same day to book the tickets. Encouragement such as this is a very blessed asset, but until one becomes aware of the symbolic language that says a lot in a little time, dreams and visions do not always appear to verify what is being done. There is much to learn and life becomes precious when tuition is taken, the way of the light becoming a really practical blessing to daily life.

Quickly arrangements were made and in one month we were on our way to Canada, there to be met with joy and a very wonderful love. There were, however, others who did not feel the same and sensitivity to this is no blessing, for one suffers pre-knowledge as well as danger in sleep. One lady in particular coveted my position. I had not really settled for sleep when in vision I saw her enter my room carrying a large earthenware urn. She stepped quickly to my bed and was about to bring the weight of the vessel down upon my head. I moved and she appeared to jerk as if being reminded about something she had forgotten. She did nothing to hurt me, but the vision did show that being covetous could be a killer.

On another occasion we were invited by friends

to lunch. Everything went well and we all enjoyed the well-prepared meal. Suddenly a terrific pain commenced to the left of my abdomen. The pain was excruciating and I leaned forward to ease myself. The pain spread, arms and legs feeling the impact. Our friends wanted to take me to a nearby hospital. I thought it better not to and asked to be allowed to lie down. I was shown to a bedroom and made comfortable in a wide bed.

Our hostess made hot tea and I was able to drink a little of it. Someone else knelt beside the bed, giving healing and encouragement to me. When all was quiet I saw a Chinese gentleman, not of this earth, come in through the door. He had a long needle resting on an enamel bowl. He did not say a word, but he pushed the needle into the seat of the pain. Immediately the violence of the pain ceased and I was comforted. "Sleep!" was the only word he said. My friends left me and I slept for some time.

I woke up with a sense of nausea, which made me leap off the bed and dash to the bathroom. It seemed as if the whole of my stomach left me almost before I could get near the toilet. When all was finished it was as if nothing had happened, for I felt wonderful. My friend who cleaned everything up was kindness itself.

How glad I was that ghosts walk and can give comfort. I have found that many will arrive at the bedside where sickness is taking its toll. Healing is accomplished where belief is sincere, love easing pain and giving full comfort. Healer and patient find a mutual unity as light brings the two onto the same level of mind. Coming to the light is sending out the warmth of love onto the ethers and so building up a force around the self. It is seen in man by the goodness in him. There is no good where kindness is neither felt nor seen.

Despite the problem of language, (this being the predominantly French-speaking province of Quebec and my command of French being poor), the word spread and a number of classes were commenced. One thing that we did find it easy to give was love, and that feeling of love moved from one to the other. Many times since then have we been uplifted with words given to us by those speaking of how love altered the whole of their lives and of others too.

32. THE TURNING POINT

The time came when I was urged to return to England. Having had to give up our rented home before we left for Canada, for a while we stayed upon our return with a friend in Uppingham Road, Leicester. Four or five months later the student who had gone with me to Canada returned there to help keep the classes together. As the classes in Leicester were doing fairly well I decided to go to North Wales, where I was made welcome by a lady who offered me her holiday flat. It was just before the Christmas of 1982 and very cold, but I was happy with the love that surrounded me. The future was hidden from me, but once again my sensitivity to underlying conditions brought me experiences, some amusing, some fearful, all of which had yet to give me further understanding.

The lady who let me stay in her holiday flat was more than kind, but she could not stop the lower type of spirit from endeavouring to break down my soul light. Even my first night there brought an experience. It had been very cold, and two friends from Leicester had taken me to North Wales with all my personal belongings. I was tired after the day's travelling and glad when night-time allowed me to retire to my warm room to find the comfort of my bed. Getting to sleep was not easy, but I was comfortable and relaxed and just beginning to lose my conscious self when suddenly I was jerked fully awake by footsteps ascending the stairs. I listened, hoping whoever was there would go away. They stopped outside my door, however, and I knew a moment of panic, and yet I could not move from my bed. I had locked the door, but slowly it opened and a man walked into the room. I breathed a sigh of relief when I saw him, for he did not appear to want to hurt me.

His hair looked damp as if he had just bathed, and his bathrobe was shabby but clean. He walked over to my bed. As he began to pull back the covers that were over me I found my voice and I gasped as I said, "What do you want?"

"You called me and I have come," he said. There was no smile.

It suddenly dawned upon me why he was there, and I searched my mind for something to say. He was very intent on getting into my bed; I was ready to jump out the other side if he succeeded. He looked at me with disbelief when I said, "I did not call. This is my bed. Go back to your wife!"

With a look of disfavour he backed away from the bed. As he went out he shut the door, the lock appearing to work by itself.

I found myself lying quietly pondering upon what had happened. My inner self had known there was a wife, and it must have spoken for me when telling him to return to her. Intuition comes from the inward part of the self and is most valuable in times of crisis.

It was then that Chang, my teacher, came in and immediately commenced speaking.

"You will be visited by many people," he said. "They usually come here for their summer holidays. Through you we shall see what is in their subconscious mind. It is not known by them that in their sleep they come here, letting us know their hidden intentions. Learn all you can, for there is much that people have not had the opportunity of learning."

Various visions and dreams appertaining to daily life followed the experience with the man in the bathrobe. I was in no hurry for others, and yet more had to come. The next was terrifying but still tuitional to me.

I was sound asleep when I was awakened by two ice-cold arms around my waist. I tried to scream, but the sound died in my throat before I could release it. It seemed I could see the individual although he was behind me. His face was distorted as if with glee. I struggled to free myself from the iron grip that held me fast. A chuckle became a cackle and I froze as his arms tightened. Despite all my pleas he would not let go. I managed to stretch out my arm and so reach the bedside light and switch it on, filling the room with light. The corpse – for it was no more than that – let me go and with a snarl it disappeared.

It was not until hearing from Chang again that I knew the full extent of mischief that could have been done. It appeared that certain people did not like my going to North Wales. Dabbling with witchery, they feared I might interfere. Up until that time I had not known to the full how far people would go in their efforts to move others away from their territory. I found out the corpse was not a being but a thought form, built up by the power of darkened thought and by design sent in my direction, possibly by a group of people. Such a creature could cause a sufficiency of fear that it could kill, and the cause of death be unknown. I was extremely grateful to eventually be able to switch on the light, a contingency not understood by the thought form, which could then go back to those who were thinking on me and could likely do damage to them, not that I would ever wish it. Such an experience I would not have believed if not suffering it, the value as a lesson therefore being great indeed.

Thanks to my numerous experiences of meeting discarnate people I shall never fear to pass from this earth plane. There is not a great deal of difference between our bodies and the bodies of people held near to the earth, this world being within the astral consciousness where everyone must eat. Should emotional conditions move one into a low state of life where light is almost non-existent, one would find that the food is very poor, having had no sunlight to help it to grow and ripen. Hard taskmasters make the work of gaining food hard and dangerous. Anyone not wanting to work is given no food and is continually exposed to the elements.

Hell is man-made. All things in the worlds unseen are thought up by man and are made by him. Darkness deepens where evil dwells, and those who protect evil people find life more than difficult. The states both of sleep and of death itself do not ease all problems; they may in fact commence more problems if the light of the soul within has been extinguished by the self or by others who murder for the sake of bloodlust. It is far worse for the killer than for the victim. Forms of death in the astral planes are perhaps worse than those in the earth. Man punishes man and no one gets away with hidden secrets, for all is exposed by where their aura takes them in sleep and in death.

I have seen that the intelligence of those who hate is very low, especially when that hate is induced by selfish desire. They might find money in the earth as astral individuals will help them, but in sleep and in death love and truth are not found by them, the whip and the rope's end being mostly their master.

The state of sleep is very revealing. Astral travel – as out of the body experience is often called – keeps one near the earth, and though exciting to a point it does not give the opportunity needed for the inner self to grow.

Bright colours in the aura take the individual into a plane of life where many other people are showing the same colour force. Happiness prevails and the soul is fed as good company increases and love is the keynote with everything each one does. Such loving people find what is called the Kingdom of Heaven within themselves; it is within because every chore is done with love and this causes it to be part of the light.

The sick are healed and the mourner finds comfort. Those hungry for righteousness are filled and they find strength, whilst the meek of the earth find succour and move into the lovely gardens of the higher planes. They find the beauty of the countryside, knowing animals and children as their companions. No one at any time in their sleep will take advantage of them.

My last experience at the holiday flat was an encounter with a man who yearned for the holidays to begin. He was very angry at finding me in the room and in the bed he thought to occupy.

"You're no good to me," he said, his voice rough with frustration.

Again my inner self gave voice. "I know that," I said. "You want a man, I think." He looked scornfully at me and disappeared through the door.

In a place where many people take their holidays, varying vibrations are induced by thought, and this can be felt by the truly sensitive.

Coming from the Midlands, the coastline of North Wales looked lovely to me. I was therefore delighted to be able to obtain a permanent flat right on the seafront, not far from my friend and her holiday flat. I know now I had to get out of my system the desire to live near the sea. Each time I have lived within sight of the sea, circumstances have been almost forced upon me from people of the earth, circumstances which have shown a lesson in disguise. Each time only the few found interest whilst others held sway over them and also over myself. My weakness was in saying yes when I should have said no. To live near the sea is no longer a desire, and I am happy to be pliable and ready to serve wherever it is necessary, my inner being giving me the insight when allowed the opportunity to lead.

It has always been possible for the brain to conceive an idea from some outside source which could stop any communication from the inward self. Whenever this has happened to me when choosing an area in which to live, the time allowed in that place has been limited. I have then had to struggle to make my way until making a choice that has really come from my inward self instead of boosting the material ideas either of myself or of someone else.

So easy is it to be waylaid that I have been caught out many times, but happily all is known and the struggle to gain strength through adversity has been watched and is of great value. Without the aid of the inner self, true progress is not known and karma is not served. Progress is the acceptance of the effects of causes commenced by the self, and through these effects the mind is able to learn truth and all that goes with it. If the soul is not allowed to do its job the brain will inadvertently use discarnate people to stand in for it.

Causes always have their following effects. In the three years or so spent in North Wales I brought myself unwittingly to a nearness of death that showed me all too clearly that in this lovely place I had been waylaid and the way I had accepted to follow was incorrect. However, some good has come out of my time there, as those who came to class have commenced a valuable work in that area. Although I had gone the incorrect way that my brain accepted, my inward self was able to turn all to good account.

◆ ◆ ◆

I did not wish to return to Leicester, but visions and sleepstates showed that I should do so. The point was made that I had to go back to retrace my steps, to pick up the threads of the correct way before being able to make any headway in the service I loved to render, teaching being the first and foremost part of my life. I know that our group could be made welcome anywhere for the numerous psychic qualities our literature brings forth, but to those who want truth and to walk the wider way wherein the inward self leads, the essential foundation lies in the teaching that is made clear and is a usable asset to daily life. So, for the sake of the tuition that is so dear to me, I accepted that my days of living in North Wales were over and that Leicester was to be my destination.

The understanding of the philosophy of true love has shown me that people who use the light of the self add light to the sun, the moon and the stars! The seasons react to the darkness of violence, hate and malice. Accidents, mishaps, sickness and death also come from this source as greed and covetousness hold sway in the subconscious mind. Man is responsible for all things appertaining to the earth life, and through man the earth must alter its mental foundation, bringing the aura of the earth from brown to sky blue. Violence of any kind, from sacrifice of human and animal bodies to war and family feuds, activates violence, be it for the sake of religion, spite or power. Each and every individual must build his own foundation by learning or tossing away tuition. All who teach other people should be the example of what they teach, thereby showing the merits of what is taught. We affect other people by our example in life; whether we serve the light or the emotional darkness of Mammon, the choice is ours and not of any god.

Being pliable, letting the inward self grow and allowing it to lead the way, one finds that fuller life will be sure. There are no props, no sacrifices, only love always knocking at the door. One has but to open the self and from the light that glows there is no limit to where one might go or to what one might do as the hours of night are passed through.

The soul being the source of light is the giver of life, and when functioning to the full is also the protector of life. The soul is fed from the light and is in complete awareness of every situation. One can prove this point when putting the best of the self into doing all necessary actions of the earth. Love sent out into the atmosphere makes every action unique. It can cause the power of love to enlarge and lead progression to its utmost fulfilment.

33. A LIFETIME OF EXPERIENCES

[Editor's Note: During her long life, Gladys had countless experiences in and out of the body, all of which helped shape her remarkable understanding of life in the earth and beyond, and of the soul's primary importance. Her autobiography includes a good number of these experiences, but there are many others that she related. Here are just a few of those episodes, giving as it were a further sample of the work that Gladys undertook to do, through which she was able to understand the finer points of the teaching.]

The Coach

I put out my hand; it does not seem to belong to me. I am awake and yet know I am asleep. My body feels light, and then it rises, following my hand. Leaving the bed I am above myself. There is a light near the wall and I make my way towards it. My heart is in my mouth, I can never get used to the thrill of going through a wall. Congratulating myself that I'm through, the lights of the streets appear below me. I am not afraid, and have no need to propel myself, for my body travels without any effort. Another adventure has begun!

A voice says, "Come," and with mounting excitement I go where I am led. I do not wonder where I am, knowing that to do so would take me back again. Only those who trust can move according to the mind. Walls are no impediment, unless the brain says, "I can't."

I look down. People are moving below, intent on getting home. Some look upwards... they are puzzled but take no further notice as they hurry on. Twilight descends and clings around everything. It is difficult to see, but fields are visible now as I look below.

My companion is urging me on, for we have work to do. He has not told me what we are going to do, his whole attention being directed to where the twilight is more pronounced than ever. Ahead of us we can see some light and are drawn towards it. There is a house, small and bright, lit with the light of love. The night could not snuff it out, and with a blessing thought we pass on our way. We do not come upon many such places, although here and there a beam of light shoots out, to fade just as quickly. The twinkling lights of electric bulbs do very little to light the way for us. The love we feel is the greater light illumining the way forward.

At last we come to a small street. Surely I recognise the houses standing in this row! And then I know I'm not mistaken, for there's my mother on the step. She is saying goodbye to her sister who is about to leave. I ponder this for a moment, because nothing has been said about my aunt coming to visit, and then again, I think to myself, 'Why is Mother out of bed?' because she hadn't been well.

A coach stands in the road, and waving goodbye to my mother, my aunt walks briskly to it and mounts the steps to sit inside. Waving once again, the coach moves off and we follow. Now I understand – we are escorts to those now leaving their earth body behind for the final time, and who are now facing the most wonderful holiday of their lives. Some may look back, and it is our job to counsel them so that they do not miss the enjoyment they have earned, for no one on this coach has hurt another person, and none has coveted anything not their own. Everyone has been hard-working though not always enjoying the job they had to do, and with wages only just adequate. But all this is in the past and to look back now, especially if with regret, can cause a yearning within oneself, and from that point it is very easy to be drawn back to earth.

You may wonder why we did not get into the coach and show ourselves, as earthly couriers would. Unfortunately it is not possible to do this, for no one must feel they are being coerced. It is our work to listen to the mind and to send in response to what is given off, so that the individual is reassured and feels no regret. Had we entered the coach it would have been an unnatural circumstance perhaps causing fear. In behaving thus unobtrusively, we were not coercing, but bringing in the good reward for what had been done in years gone by.

The people look happy enough. The older ones are used to riding in a coach, so it is all quite ordinary to them. One lady has a child on her lap, and is looking at it with wondering eyes. It has been many years since her love was so stirred. As we watch the light spread all around her, we exchange a smile, knowing her love will lead her to care for little children, not to be lonely or sad any more.

Gradually a different atmosphere begins to pervade the coach, when a man says testily, "Why doesn't this so-and-so coach go faster?" He had not had to covet a drink before, having been a publican. Now liquor is beyond his reach and we sigh, for his future is also assured. Once again he will find a pub and be happy pulling up the pints, but as to whether he will want this to last indefinitely, one cannot say. To be satisfied in one way does not mean there will be happiness in every way.

Each person is being led in a different way. No one knows that the inner body is approaching a new life. The old body being left behind, the journey is not like any taken previously, yet from what is said by each we gather that the changeover has been entirely unrecognisable. Chattering is now interspersed with pointed remarks, some of the older people being irritated by the length of the journey. Thinking about the need to get out of the coach is overriding the fact that the body is no longer pressing its needs. The agitation becomes so strong that mind communication is impeded, so make our way into the coach to be in closer contact. Having now travelled some way, we find this possible, because the collective consciousness has dropped so low that in comparison we are invisible.

Every irritating remark brings added darkness, striking the minds of everyone else, because no one is strong enough to stop it. Almost immediately, however, we see a flickering light here and there, as a battle goes on in the minds of those who do not want to get depressed. We draw nearer to each whose light is flickering, impressing on them the need to be patient and to enjoy the ride. It is a pleasure to watch the response, as, flinging back the head, each one seems to throw off a burden, and looking round with a smile, begins to alter the collective mind to the benefit of those who are receptive.

Just as this is happening, the coach stops. The destination has not been called out, yet some people are saying goodbye. With a word to the driver, each alights, having eyes only for what they can find for themselves. Relations and friends are waiting, surprising though this may seem, for the ways of life are not really known, and the possibilities beyond the limited physical body have yet to be fully understood. It is known however that the subconscious mind makes all the arrangements, sometimes drawing good or not-so-good people to receive the newcomers.

You may think it a stupid thing for the subconscious mind to attract not-so-good people, but consider the muddled consciousness; it is then possible to see that patience and tolerance are in perpetual combat with low emotions, drawing adverse conditions as the body's needs make their demands.

Visiting other planes of consciousness during sleep is not unnatural, and when eventually the last journey is taken, there need be no unhappiness to mar the passing. At first the pull of the earth is not felt, but when relatives and friends left behind mourn, most travellers sense the pain and can be held in one position without full enjoyment of either one plane of life or the other.

Mourning for a long time is disruptive, and automatically the link of love dries up. Then the one is not allowed to wait for the other, for in this case love turns to possession, and possessiveness turns to selfishness. It can do nothing more than attend upon its own state of consciousness. This releases the oppressed, unless they wish to linger. Few do, when the truth is made known to them and they can see the reaction of the one left behind, for many of earth fulfil bodily pleasures to bring forgetfulness, little realising as to how the mind reacts.

Love never possesses, it allows release, so that happiness might come to the one loved. There is nothing that one wants to forget when full love continues, for service in one way or another keeps love alive, the blessing of this coming when the earth body lies asleep. Anyone who mourns a loved one and is true to them can meet the beloved in the night. Spending happy hours in conversation, love is enlarged, and when the time for passing comes, it is then quite natural to be with each other and continue to serve.

Finding pleasurable pursuits can so fill the mind, that although love is thought to be uppermost, it is not. Pleasures continue throughout the night, and when this happens there is no possibility of knowing the truth of love.

On our coach there are two ladies and one gentleman whose love is to be amply repaid. They get off at the next stop and welcoming arms are raised to help them. Now we have only a few passengers left. The coach was full when we started out, and the few yet remaining do not seem to mind where they are going, being quite content to sit and wait. They watch the panoramic scenery – for it almost seems that the coach is standing still. The fields are brilliant with flowers, and colour abounds everywhere. Light radiates, and happiness is transmitted from one to another, enfolding all in a mental warmth.

The grass is a glorious green, fresh and bright. I listen while my aunt whispers to her neighbour, "I do believe we're going home! I lived in the country when I was a girl, and I've never forgotten it." While she is speaking, the coach slows down and comes to a stop, then she and the remaining passengers alight. We notice a woman in a soft gown gracefully walking towards the coach. She passes smilingly from one to another, until she comes to the one standing apart – the frail-looking woman nursing a child, soon to find out she's been taken there to be a children's nurse. First she will undergo a short period of rest and rejuvenation to regain her youth and to lose any weighty thoughts that are the product of her time in earth. I have seen this happen many times when the inward self undergoes revitalisation. Colour plays a very active part in the process.

The rest of the passengers move towards a group of people standing by tables spread with refreshments and other good things. I notice that fruits of the trees are most in evidence, and there is nothing cooked at all. No one else appears to remark upon this, but laughing and talking together they are lost in enjoyment. Having finished our escorting assignment my companion and I walk away, the handshaking and laughter not for us – for we are not really there! With the sound of many voices in my ears, I wake up in my own bed.

I have had many such experiences before, so did not question as to whether the whole thing had been just a dream. It has been borne in on me for many years that there is far more significance in dreams than most people care to admit. Anyone seriously investigating the state of sleep and the various planes of consciousness to which one can go, cannot fail to discover the reality of life out of the body. Over the long years of research, I have come to rely more and more on the inner consciousness and its rehearsal of fact before it takes place on the earth. It prepares me for much that could be a shock to the system, and when happiness is near, the prelude to it is as joyous as the actual event. Free will is not tampered with, for at no time is one's will restricted. By this I know that nothing is fixed or predetermined in any way.

The hours of night slid behind me and I grew impatient to get up and see my mother, whom I felt must be made aware of what I had experienced. What I did not taken into account was that she was just as versed in dreams as I was, and when I was able to go to see her, she told me about her sister's visit, and the coach stopping at the gate. "Just as if she had come calling," she said. My aunt's passing from earth had not yet happened, but we knew then that it would not be long before we would hear the news of it.

'Ah,' you may be thinking, 'that's just the point; like mother, like daughter.' Many people are misled by thinking thus, for all who sincerely seek find, and for that matter, those who are insincere must find also. They find in their own way, which is often far from pleasing, but this is the natural schooling one receives.

Healing

Most of us tend to do a lot of thinking about various things when we are left alone with nothing to occupy our brain or our hands. From such thoughts I came to ponder upon past help and the experiences from which comfort had been found.

Three most wonderful healing experiences came to mind. How well I still remember these times of joy. Upon each of these occasions I awoke from sleep and being fully conscious I was able to observe all that was happening. These psychic operations were the most natural experiences I have had.

In the first case those of Spirit removed fibroids, saving me from an operation which would have led to much distress. Before the operation I woke to see a nurse bending over me. She then went to check the steriliser. I remember that steam came out as she lifted up the lid. A surgeon was scrubbing up at a basin. My bedroom, which had no basin, was more like an operating theatre but I could see that it was still my room.

Both surgeon and nurse worked without looking at my face. I felt no pain whatsoever. When all was finished I laughed as the surgeon threw the towel for the nurse to catch. Both of them were very much at ease, feeling no tension at any time. Tiredness was unknown at that moment. The efforts during the night had not only stimulated myself, but these two wonderful people as well. Their life and work in the earth plane had ceased but their joy was still in giving service to pained bodies. There was nothing about them which frightened, only complete blessing and happiness was felt in their presence.

The second healing was that of arthritis. It came at a time when the pain in my knees was almost unbearable and I found myself frantically calling for help. The way in which the help came was not surgery performed by a spirit doctor, or even a psychic operation in the truest sense. However, to me it was the love of the Spirit that was operating. I say this because in answer to my plea a young woman appeared. She carried a large book and, opening it at the side of my bed, she ran her finger down the list of names in it. Nodding her head at what she found she pointed her forefinger at my knees. The pain ceased immediately. I was so bemused by what had happened that I hardly noticed the going of my benefactress. She left so quickly and quietly that there was no opportunity for me to give her my thanks; indeed she did not appear to want any from me. Such love is often beyond our comprehension and yet in striving to find it we gain benefit and blessing.

❖ ❖ ❖

In thinking upon this theme of healing, I would like to mention the first really high level of consciousness, where people go who serve and have a hard time in the earth, picking up sickness as the light from them is made low. They can be taken as I was to a hospital in this plane of life, which is mostly for healing workers who use the soul, not for people who use psychic power.

On the earth I had served a church on a bitter cold day, a message telling me not to come because of the bad weather did not reach me. I had to go by coach and I had bronchitis. It was a place I had visited before and they had complained of mediums who let them down at the last minute.

The coach had no heating and arriving at the church I found no one about. After half an hour a lady came, it was very close to the time of commencing the afternoon meeting. I had been travelling for three hours but found nowhere open where I could get a cup of tea and something to eat. As this led me to the wonderful experience I had, I say no more of it. I will say, however, that the eight people who did come to the service were very appreciative, and that made an excellent atmosphere in which to talk to them. It was very cold but we tried to be happy and keep warm with the Spirit.

It was late when I got back home and went straight to bed. The next day the doctor came and diagnosed pneumonia, which meant I had to stay in bed.

That night was the loveliest night I feel I have ever had. At 8 p.m. an elderly lady came into my room. She said, "I will be with you all night, you will be going to hospital."

"I am not going to hospital, my family will look after me," I replied.

The lady smiled and said, "Sleep!" She was kind but firm and knew what she was talking about, for in my sleep my inner body was taken from my bed. I went some distance and felt I was floating on air.

Arriving at the hospital I was taken to a ward where a nurse met me and quickly made me welcome. As I was sitting up in bed, the nurse smiled and said, "Look, you have friends here already." Three letters she gave me, but I could not remember afterwards who they were from. The next morning I woke in my bed, knowing nothing of the journey home. The lady was sitting by the fire, and yet I knew there was no fire in the grate. She had been doing some sewing and putting her work away in a basket she said, "Good morning," to me and left. I would have loved to talk to her and hoped I would see her again. As she left, the fire went out and the chair she had been sitting on vanished.

For three nights the lady came and sat by my sleeping self while I went to that hospital. When I left the hospital I had been reading a book. As I left it on the bed I said, "That is a jolly good book," and woke up in my own bed feeling wonderful and able to get up.

When the doctor returned he said, "You are better. How could that happen?" He was puzzled but I did not enlighten him. "Call me if you get worse again," he said. I had no need to call him, relying far more upon the light than upon the doctor's medicine, which I did not take.

So many times have such things happened to me, that I could never close my eyes to the authenticity of the love that comes when one serves and is made low by that service.

Late For An Appointment

It has been my joy to talk to the elderly, many of whom feel acutely their lack of physical activity. Preparing for the great day of leaving the body, can bring surprise upon surprise. But not only the deathbed opens one to seeing into two worlds at one and the same time, for when asleep, one can share in the life yet to be. The wisdom of keeping the subconscious mind active has not been taught, people taking it for granted that death overtakes the body without preparation of any kind. Unhappiness, however, is the outcome if the subconscious does not know its way.

Many can be frightened and stop happiness coming to them if they block progress by hanging on to the earth life, no matter how feeble the link is.

It does not matter how old or infirm the body

is, the inner self can be quite different. Similar in shape it may be, but beyond that, its organism and appearance are subject to the mind and all that is rooted in it. The elderly can take on new life, and the sunshine of happiness need not be weighed in terms of how much money they have, when the inner body can find perfect pleasure – and all without cost! Sitting in a chair puts chains on those who accept them, but for those who are inwardly free, there are no chains that can hold them prisoner. Travelling over land and sea in the inner body is a delight that I would not forego for anything on this earth, and it can be exactly the same for people who have only scant life forces and seemingly little to live for. So enjoyable can such travel become that to stay in bed is a pleasure instead of the bind it might be.

Vanity and personal desire will bring nothing to bless, but those who give themselves and mentally hold on to nothing worldly, will find blessing in higher planes, where peace of mind is held. Relatives and friends are reunited in sleep, joining in parties and picnics. Hanging too much on home, or family ties, the new revelation cannot be experienced; happy times are not found and perhaps the release will not take full effect until many years after the body is discarded altogether. What is thought and felt before passing becomes stronger as the inner body clings to all that has been valued – causing an individual to be earthbound.

Once, when I was to travel out of the body to Mexico, I was two minutes late going to my chair in the afternoon. My physical brain had not known of the work myself and another companion were to do. When we arrived at a lovely house with its surrounding patio, the servant spoke severely to me, saying: "You are two minutes late. Madam is angry she has had to be kept waiting."

The lady had passed over and had been kept in the house pending our arrival, for we were to accompany her to her new life. She had been a querulous type, apt to blame others for the least action that put her out, so we had to take her where this trait could be ironed out.

As we walked past some large houses, she said, "We needn't go any further, one of these will do for me."

I looked at her and stood still for a moment. "Do you believe you are going to be given a house like this when you have never given anything away in your life?"

She looked at me stonily. "I can buy it, can't I?" she asked somewhat crossly.

"Money does not change hands here," I said. "It is some way to go. We shall have to leave you if you do not hurry."

After passing some smaller houses we came to a hut. I opened the door and the woman stepped back in dismay.

"I can't live here. Look, everything is broken!"

"That is because you only gave away broken things. All you have given is here for you to use. To grumble now will only make things worse. Learn to love and give; you will not find servants here, and no one will help you because of the way you treated those who had to work for you on the earth. It is up to you to be appreciative, that perhaps could be a help, but no doubt it will be a while before people will trust you. Or you can go back to the earth, except this time there would be no money and you will have to work hard as you have made your servants work. There will be help for you only when you have learned to willingly help other people."

At this she commenced to weep. "I cannot manage on my own," she wailed.

I found myself gradually slipping away, but said, "I think you should try and not expect someone else to do it for you. You will find you have to eat here also, so you might have to work."

She could not see me, but said loudly, "I shall die first!"

I smiled at that and found I was back in my chair but have never forgotten that incident. I hope she has since tried to help herself without getting angry or frustrated, for she would get help if she has. I could not tell her this but asked that she might be shown the way. We were allowed to accompany the lady, for the shock to her was great, and everyone is given the opportunity to bless another before being sent where they must find the will to learn. If at the last moment they express outgoing love, thus cutting the tie with earth and all that was part of it, a place in a holiday camp is reached, so that for a while they can enjoy the company of others while the new inner love is growing and taking root.

When money has a bearing on the mind before passing, the inner self will also need it to continue its life, food being as much a problem as on the earth. Unfortunately she was set in her ways and could not easily change. The time may be long when all at once she might open her eyes and see what is good for herself; immediately she would feel the warmth of love around her. Meanwhile, her own comfort must lie in the way she might think and feel from her inward self that holds the power of change.

The Sheik

It is an excellent idea to sit or lie down for a period of time every day, just giving the self over to quietness - or as some would say, to God. Lovely places can be visited, where no language barrier halts the pleasure of communication. Before being set to writing I gave two hours each day to the Spirit, my main objective being to learn all I could about life, both in and out of the body. My most colourful trip was out into the desert, where the whole afternoon was spent in the harem of a Bedouin sheik. He was seated upon numerous cushions; the beautiful young ladies appeared very happy to sit round him. I was teaching them of the philosophy written for the tuition of my students. They were all greatly intrigued by the way I had learned and what I could pass on to them.

The colour of everything was breathtaking, but time sped by and all too soon I had to return to my body. With a deep sigh I left the lovely scene, but only after a promise had been extracted from me that I would come again and speak more about the ways of the Spirit. It might seem to some inquiring minds that nothing of lasting worth can come from such travel. But having seen the outcome of some of my journeys I have no doubt that great benefit can result, affecting not only those who receive the spoken word, but all others with whom they come into daily contact.

Sometimes two or three places are visited during the same night. I do not know all that happens while I am sleeping. But what it is good for me to remember I invariably find coming back to me, even a day or so later when some incident starts the subconscious giving off all that has been stored.

Pen and paper on the bedside table act as an incentive to the inner self to give of what is there, and on the point of waking one may remember enough to make a note of any experience. Leaving it until one gets up, however, will often cause forgetfulness, much value being missed thereby.

GLADYS FRANKLIN

AFTERWORD

In this autobiography, Gladys details significant chapters in her life up to when she is a little over eighty years old. The last stage of her life, a period of ten years not covered by her autobiography, is just as interesting. During this time the organisation she founded for both research and for teaching began to operate under the new name of *Studies on Life*, in order to reflect a change in emphasis from philosophy classes to smaller, more self-sufficient study groups.

Gladys continued to write extensively upon her subject, writings designed more for sincere study than for casual reading. Included in her output were three totally separate courses of study lessons, each consisting of thirty lesson papers and thirty audio tapes. Always wanting to give her students and followers the very best of her teaching, and to encourage them not to hold on to lesser ideas from the past, she suggested that only the last of these series of lessons be made available to the general public. This last series, written in the final year of her life, gives a true summary of many of the most important things she learned through first-hand experience. It is entitled 'The Scene Today', because it presents a full understanding of how to enhance the value of the soul in the context of today's world. (If you wish to know more then please see the section on *Other Books and Links* at the end of this book.)

In 1993 Gladys married again. Roger, her second husband, was utterly sincere in his devotion to Gladys and to the work of the Spirit, and by virtue of his support Gladys was able to complete all she had set out to do. Their civil wedding ceremony was followed by a spiritual wedding at which I was honoured to be the officiant.

Gladys at her desk

Gladys was a prolific letter writer, continually in correspondence with people such as myself who were interested in her work. Her letters, all beautifully handwritten, were often pages and pages long, giving personal news and an update on the work, as well as helpful bits of clairvoyance and teaching, and perhaps a printed copy of a paper she had only just written. The photograph of Gladys writing at her desk, in what would be the last year of her life in the earth, is one of my favourite reminders of her.

Chang, Gladys' own spirit teacher, once said that the Masters in Spirit had told him he would never find anyone on earth to work with him to bring the Project of the Golden Ball forward. They said it couldn't be done. Against all the odds he found Gladys, someone who proved herself willing to learn and to always put the Spirit first. Chang went on to say that he was not able to find anyone else – she was the only one.

Gladys passed peacefully into the world of Spirit in March 2000 at the age of ninety-one. Since then she has continued her work in the school of which she is the principal, in a plane far higher than the earth. This is the school she was promised for completing her work in the earth, where pupils are taught how to build their own soul light. It has over five thousand students.

Some of her followers, including myself, have been fortunate enough to experience meeting her again, and to visit her school. Today, the trustees of Studies of Life carry on the work of making available her philosophical writings and her novels, all of which contain a strong thread of tuition for the wider life.

In addition, Gladys continues to encourage

those still in the earth plane who are seeking the light. Only very recently she was walking alongside me in a sleepstate, telling me to watch my dreams closely. And as we have learned from reading her autobiography, watching and taking note of our dreams and experiences is a good way of understanding our inward self – to bring heaven and earth together, as it were, for a happier, more peaceful, and more fulfilling life. May this fulfilment be for you my friend, whoever you are and wherever you may be.

Editor

OTHER BOOKS AND LINKS

And Some Have Mansions: A novel by **Gladys Franklin**, based upon her own out-of-body adventures, available as a kindle ebook on Amazon. In the aftermath of a coach crash the passengers begin their journey into the afterlife. Have you ever wondered where we go after transition or if it possible to visit people in other planes of life? Find out as life unfolds for each of the crash victims, in unseen worlds above and below the earth.

www.studiesonlife.com: A comprehensive website and blog devoted entirely to the teachings of Gladys Franklin, maintained by two of her students.

Soul Lore: Discovering the inner self and the soul: A narrative by **C. E. Jones**, available in both paperback and kindle ebook format on Amazon. A book that answers fundamental questions about life, death, and the afterlife, written by the editor of Gladys Franklin's autobiography. Soul Lore is the esoteric teaching that encourages spiritual development through awareness of the secret inner self.

www.cejonesauthor.com: A website and blog inspired by the teachings of Gladys Franklin, maintained by C. E. Jones, a lifetime student of her philosophy.

Printed in Great Britain
by Amazon

56804713R00139